ORGANIZING AND CLEANING STRATEGIES FOR ADHD

QUICK AND TAILORED TECHNIQUES TO DECLUTTER YOUR SPACE, OPTIMIZE YOUR WORKSTATION, AND BOOST PRODUCTIVITY FOR A STRESS-FREE LIFE

LATRICIA MAY

© Copyright Latricia May 2024- All rights reserved.

The content within this book may not be reproduced, duplicated or transmitted without direct written permission from the author or the publisher.

Under no circumstances will any blame or legal responsibility be held against the publisher, or author, for any damages, reparation, or monetary loss due to the information contained within this book. Either directly or indirectly. You are responsible for your own choices, actions, and results.

Legal Notice:

This book is copyright protected. This book is only for personal use. You cannot amend, distribute, sell, use, quote or paraphrase any part, of the content within this book, without the consent of the author or publisher.

Disclaimer Notice:

Please note the information contained within this document is for educational and entertainment purposes only. All effort has been expended to present accurate, up-to-date, and reliable, complete information. No warranties of any kind are declared or implied. Readers acknowledge that the author is not engaging in the rendering of legal, financial, medical or professional advice. The content within this book has been derived from various sources. Please consult a licensed professional before attempting any techniques outlined in this book.

By reading this document, the reader agrees that under no circumstances is the author responsible for any losses, direct or indirect, which are incurred as a result of the use of the information contained within this document, including, but not limited to, — errors, omissions, or inaccuracies.

CONTENTS

Introduction — 5

1. DECODING ADHD-THE SCIENCE AND THE STORIES — 9
The Brain's Wiring: How to View ADHD through the Lens of Neurodiversity — 10
How ADHD Fits into the Neurodiverse Spectrum — 11
Debunking Myths about ADHD and Intelligence — 13
Understanding the Science of ADHD: Diagnosis, Presentations, and Genetic and Environmental Factors — 14
Unpacking the ADHD Mindset: How Neurodivergent People See the World Differently — 24

2. THE CHAOS OF CLUTTER NAVIGATING ADHD'S ORGANIZATIONAL MINEFIELD — 33
Understand the Connection between Clutter and ADHD — 33
Untangling the Emotional Side of Clutter: Erasing Shame by Focusing on Function over Perfection — 36
Setting up ADHD-Friendly Systems to Prevent and Reduce Clutter — 39
How to Cope with Procrastination: Strategies to Overcome Procrastination and Action Paralysis — 45

3. ROOM BY ROOM REBOOT CUSTOM ORGANIZING FOR EVERY SPACE — 49
Kitchen Command Center: Cooking up Order — 49
Creating Healthy, Sustainable, and ADHD-Friendly Cooking and Meal-Prepping Routines — 52
Living Room Oasis: Decluttering for Leisure — 57
Bedroom Bliss: Crafting Calm in Private Quarters — 60
Bathroom Sanctuary: Streamlining Self-Care — 63

4. DECLUTTER YOUR DESK, OPTIMIZE YOUR WORKING STATION TO REDUCE STRESS AND ENHANCE PRODUCTIVITY WITH ADHD-FRIENDLY PLANNING — 71
Crafting Your ADHD-Friendly Workspace — 72
The Unique Challenges of Remote Work: How to Get Work Done at Home — 74
Digital Declutter: Managing Your Virtual Workspace — 79
How to Reach Your Goals One Step at a Time by Crafting an ADHD-Friendly Planner — 84

5. SOCIAL SYNC NAVIGATING ADHD IN YOUR SOCIAL SPHERE — 91
Getting Organized and Preparing for Social Engagements — 92
How to Navigate Sensory Overload and Feelings of Overwhelm in Social Settings — 94
How to Reshape Social Circles and Create Meaningful Engagements — 97
Social Synching in Your Romantic Life: Why Awareness and Acceptance of Your ADHD Is Crucial — 103

6. CRAFTING CALM FROM CHAOS ADHD-FRIENDLY ROUTINES FOR A STRESSFREE LIFE — 107
Habit Stacking: The Foundation of Daily Triumphs — 108
Tailoring Tasks to Energy Levels: Work with Your ADHD, Not Against It — 112
The Role of Morning Routines in Getting You Started for the Day — 115
Evening Wind Down: Preparing for Tomorrow — 116

Conclusion — 125
Endnotes — 129

INTRODUCTION

When your home is a mess, you feel like a mess.

A place doesn't feel like home if you aren't deeply connected to it. You paint the walls the way you like, buy the right furniture, and organize it perfectly across the rooms while decorating each living space with gifts, trinkets, personal mementos, and cherished items.

Feeling guilt, shame, and disappointment isn't a surprise when all your effort is overshadowed by dust on every surface, dirty clothes on the furniture, items all over the floor, and an overflowing kitchen sink.

This is also how I felt when I couldn't keep my house in order.

I felt ashamed because I had a successful career and a thriving family. Everywhere in life, I was either on top of my game or capable enough to make it work, but keeping my home clean felt impossible. It was humiliating to think that the seemingly easiest of them all was the hardest.

For years, I tried every method on Earth, from niche strategies you'd find in small blogs to mainstream systems from best-selling books. Despite the encyclopedia of knowledge I had, the situation turned better only after my ADHD diagnosis.

Until my ADHD diagnosis, I felt like a puzzle that had lost a piece somewhere along the way. I could swear that multiple voices in my head urged me toward opposing and contradictory actions.

It turns out that ADHD has been shown to significantly impair your ability to consistently do household chores, based on a study of more than 800 people.[1] ADHD also makes procrastination worse and increases your forgetfulness, like not remembering where you left your keys, phone, wallet, and other important items.[2]

Every ADHD symptom, from distractibility and poor impulse control to lack of motivation and disorganization, had been making it hard to keep my home clean and clutter-free. Knowing there was an underlying cause behind my immense challenges wasn't an excuse but a much-needed explanation.

If you are reading this, you may be recently diagnosed and hungry for solutions, or maybe you're even a seasoned ADHD veteran who's tired and desperate for some advice when nothing else has worked.

No matter your circumstances, you are aware that knowing how your ADHD makes organization harder isn't the same as knowing how to fix it. A diagnosis makes it clear what you are up against, but the clarity you get is only a small part of the solution.

This was a painful lesson I had to learn through years of costly errors and mistakes. The book in front of you is the result of my struggles. It consists of all the hard-earned wisdom I've accumulated over the years, written so you can go through the same journey more smoothly.

If I had to describe the book in two words, they would be "holistic" and "comprehensive."

Throughout the book, I unpack all the sources of clutter and disorganization in the ADHD household from multiple angles and offer solutions that address not only the strategies and systems you can use but also the underlying beliefs, attitudes, and assumptions you may have about the process. You will be encouraged to change the tools you use to keep your home in order and the way you think about the organization from the ground up.

Finally, the book goes beyond staying organized by offering strategies for all areas of life that can impact your ability to keep your home clean, organized, and clutter-free. Keeping your house clean and tidy also depends on your performance at work, the health of your social life, the consistency of your self-care routines, and the habits and routines that keep you happy, balanced, and free of stress.

If you are ready for an ADHD-friendly, sustainable, and shame-free approach to organizing your home and your life, let's get started.

CHAPTER 1
DECODING ADHD-THE SCIENCE AND THE STORIES

If you have recently been diagnosed or even if you've known about your condition for years, understanding attention deficit hyperactivity disorder can be a huge challenge.

Despite the ADHD label defining a strict set of symptoms, the wide variety of presentations and unique lived experiences prove that trying to confine the ADHD experience to a single label is simplistic at best and reductionist at worst.

This chapter will explore what it means to have ADHD while debunking common stereotypes and misconceptions. By combining insights from the people who live with the condition and the conclusions of the largest studies done over multiple years, you will receive a comprehensive overview of what ADHD is, how it affects your daily life, and the most common and time-tested strategies you can use to manage it.

THE BRAIN'S WIRING: HOW TO VIEW ADHD THROUGH THE LENS OF NEURODIVERSITY

If you have ADHD, you are a person who's neurodivergent. This means that the way you process information, manage your emotions, think, and navigate the world around you differs from most of the population.

The concept of neurodivergence emerged from the neurodiversity movement, which states that human brains have a wide variety and diversity in their internal world (thoughts, feelings, and sensations), behavior around other people, and just in general.

People are wildly different, and there's nothing wrong with that.

Much like we don't judge people based on the color of their skin, hair, and eyes, we also shouldn't be making judgments about the unique ways through which people experience the world and navigate everyday life. From communication skills and style to creativity, self-awareness, and mind-body connection, there are countless criteria we can use to measure the differences in people's cognitions.

Neurodiversity advocates want to make the idea of being neurodivergent more morally neutral.

Currently, there is a stigma against people with attention deficit hyperactivity disorder (ADHD), autism spectrum disorder (ASD), sensory processing disorders (SPD), and other people who don't fit into traditional norms of thinking and behaving. If you diverge from social norms, stigma and offensive labels (crazy, crippled, disabled, and mentally ill) are common.

Making neurodivergence more morally neutral means reducing the hatred and outrage toward those different from the majority.

Being different doesn't mean there is anything wrong with you. In fact, neurodiversity is something we ought to cherish.

After all, many of history's greatest achievements come from people who are non-conformist thinkers with out-of-the-box ideas and creative projects. Diversity in human cognition makes life richer and more meaningful for everyone because we learn from the unique viewpoints and wisdom of those different from us.

HOW ADHD FITS INTO THE NEURODIVERSE SPECTRUM

Let's imagine a scale from one to ten and use it to measure the alertness and ability to concentrate between two different people.

One means the person struggles to keep their focus in one place for longer than a few seconds. Ten means the person can stay concentrated for as long as they want while ignoring background noises, distracting thoughts, and disturbing feelings.

If you have ADHD, you are more likely to be at the lower end of the attention spectrum. You will also likely get a similarly low rating for impulse control, organizational skills, time awareness, and many other mental skills required to effectively navigate everyday life.

Using a scale to roughly measure someone's cognitive traits and abilities is crucial because your score can make the difference between an uncomfortable cognitive trait and a severe symptom of a disorder that significantly disrupts your life. A neurotypical person (someone without ADHD) can also get distracted, procrastinate, and make impulsive decisions from time to time, but if those traits are not frequent and painful enough, they are not enough to classify this behavior as a disorder.

Calling ADHD a disorder is not ideal but necessary in today's society because you get protection from discrimination in the workplace, special accommodation programs by the government, and a host of other resources to help you cope and manage your condition. In a world full of misinformation and ignorance surrounding mental health, the ADHD label allows us to clearly draw a line between someone with a slight problem and someone who definitely needs professional help.

Still, the label of "disorder" doesn't come without side effects. When you focus on the negative impact that ADHD symptoms have on your life, it becomes easier to think of yourself as flawed and imperfect. This is why looking at your condition through a neurodiversity lens can help you better understand yourself and your ADHD.

Being neurodivergent means you are simply different, not broken in any way. Furthermore, neurodiversity goes beyond deficits, difficulties, challenges, and negative symptoms. Many ADHD experts and neurodivergent people report greater creativity, empathy, intuitive decision-making, ability to work under stress, and other strengths unique to ADHD.[1]

Finally, neurodiversity helps us remember that there are key differences, even in people diagnosed with ADHD.

Clinically speaking, those differences can lead to different presentations of the condition, which we will discuss later in this chapter. For now, you should know that two people with the same ADHD diagnosis can struggle with different symptoms and will likely have different strengths based on their personality, interests, life history, and past and current environments.

DEBUNKING MYTHS ABOUT ADHD AND INTELLIGENCE

Despite the rates of ADHD diagnosis and awareness growing every single year, the stigma behind the condition remains strong. One of the most widespread misconceptions about ADHD is that it correlates with lower intelligence. Let's look at why people with ADHD don't actually have low intelligence and why many of the challenges they go through don't have anything to do with IQ.

The easiest way to measure intelligence is through IQ since it is easily quantifiable. However, the data here is still controversial. Some studies suggest no difference that is statistically significant in ADHD rates among children of different IQ groups. Still, other large studies suggest that people with ADHD are on the lower end of the average intelligence range. So, if the average range is 90 to 109, those with ADHD may be more likely to be in the lower bracket of this range.[2]

At first glance, this is slightly concerning, even if the difference is marginal. However, keep in mind that there are obvious problems with the design of those studies. Russell Barkley, world-renowned ADHD expert and psychiatrist, points out that it's hard to objectively evaluate the intelligence of a person when they have ADHD symptoms.[3]

Since ADHD makes you more likely to zone out, get distracted, make impulsive decisions, lose track of time, and struggle with visualization, the IQ score on a test may be lower than what you are capable of. This is one of the most common and painful problems with ADHD—you can be immensely talented, intelligent, and capable, but your symptoms prevent you from turning this potential into reality and your intentions into action.

This gap between what you are capable of doing and what you end up doing has to do with many ADHD symptoms leading to procrastination, disorganization, impaired self-control, lack of motivation, distractability, and inability to pay attention.

The negative impact of ADHD doesn't end with lower scores on some IQ tests.

Often, people with ADHD are accused of not caring enough, being lazy, and irresponsible for struggling to do daily tasks. When your disorder remains undiagnosed or you are in the presence of people who don't understand ADHD, symptoms of the condition can be mistaken for personal choices and character failures, even if the two are separate.

You don't consciously choose to work only at the last moment, leave your house without cleaning for weeks, or completely forget about the food in the fridge before it expires. ADHD symptoms, especially when not treated and managed, can significantly impair your ability to do tasks. Other people don't see this battle going on in your head, which is why it's easy for them to judge and critique you.

UNDERSTANDING THE SCIENCE OF ADHD: DIAGNOSIS, PRESENTATIONS, AND GENETIC AND ENVIRONMENTAL FACTORS

Here is what we know about ADHD based on the current scientific consensus:

- ADHD is a neurodevelopmental disorder leading to delays of up to 30 percent in the development of various mental skills, like organization, task initiation, and concentration.[4]
- ADHD causes delays in the growth of the prefrontal cortex and a reduction in gray matter density in various brain regions.[5]

- ADHD is associated with abnormalities in the function of dopamine, norepinephrine, and, to a lesser extent, serotonin, which are brain chemicals responsible for mental skills like attention, motivation, and impulse control.[6]
- ADHD runs in families, so in the majority of cases, you inherit genes from your parents that lead to the development of ADHD. But, you can also get it as a result of brain damage and injury in the womb, early childhood, and even in adulthood (rare cases).[7]
- No matter the cause of ADHD, an official diagnosis means you have differences in brain function that are permanent and irreversible.
- Healthy eating and nutrition management, regular aerobic and strength exercises, mindfulness exercises, and a host of other lifestyle changes can reduce the severity of ADHD symptoms, but they can never cure them entirely.[8] [9]

There is still much for us to learn about the origins of ADHD. Thankfully, this doesn't stop the diagnosis and treatment of the condition because the symptoms people report and clinicians observe remain the same, no matter the underlying cause.

Although there are differences in the exact phrasing and criteria requirement, most diagnosis examinations require an evaluation of a person's behavior in two primary domains: inattention and hyperactivity.

For instance, the fifth edition of the Diagnostic and Statistical Manual of Mental Disorders (DSM-5) in the US requires children to have more than six symptoms (more than five for adults) for either inattention or hyperactive-impulsive behavior.

Inattention Symptoms, According to the DSM-5:[10]

- Often fails to give close attention to details or makes careless mistakes in schoolwork, work, or other activities
- Often has difficulty sustaining attention in tasks or play activities
- Often does not seem to listen when spoken to directly
- Often does not follow through on instructions and fails to finish schoolwork, chores, or duties in the workplace
- Often has difficulty organizing tasks and activities
- Often avoids, dislikes, or is reluctant to engage in tasks that require sustained mental effort
- Often loses things necessary for tasks or activities
- Is often easily distracted by extraneous stimuli
- Is often forgetful in daily activities

Impulsivity-Hyperactivity Symptoms, According to the DSM-5:

- Often fidgets with or taps hands or feet or squirms in seat
- Often leaves seat in situations when remaining seated is expected
- Often runs about or climbs in situations where it is inappropriate
- Often unable to play or engage in leisure activities quietly
- Often behaves like they are "on the go", acting as if "driven by a motor"
- Often talks excessively
- Often blurts out an answer before a question has been completed
- Often has difficulty waiting their turn
- Often interrupts or intrudes on others

On top of the score you get in each category, an ADHD diagnosis also requires the following requirements to be met:

- Frequency: The DSM-5 intentionally puts "often" in front of every symptom because having ADHD suggests that you experience negative side effects to your mental health and everyday life frequently, and not as one-time events or infrequent episodes.
- Cross-Setting Occurrence: The DSM-5 requires ADHD symptoms to show up in multiple diverse settings, like at home, school, university, work, with friends, and another social environment, since it increases the chance that the symptoms are caused by ADHD and not by any environmental problems.
- Corroboration: Many clinicians will require self-reporting on questionnaires and insights from close family, friends, and co-workers to minimize bias. This is because how people see themselves may not accurately reflect their everyday behavior as seen by the people around them.
- Exclusion of Other Possible Disorders: Inattention and a lack of impulse control are common in many mental health disorders like BPD, OCD, anxiety, clinical depression, psychosis, and others, so another diagnosis must be ruled out to ensure you are not wrongly diagnosed with ADHD while your symptoms are caused by something else.
- Early Childhood Onset: The DSM-5 requires ADHD symptoms to be present before the age of 12, which is supposed to be another measurement of how the condition persists despite the vast differences in how you live. Unfortunately, this is one of the outdated requirements since, in many adolescents, symptoms may

not be clearly visible until much later, especially if they are dominantly inattentive symptoms.

Depending on how many symptoms resonate within each category, you will receive a different presentation of ADHD. Resonating with mostly inattention symptoms results in an inattentive ADHD presentation, resonating with mostly hyperactive symptoms leads to a predominantly hyperactive-impulsive, and an equal distribution leads to a combined presentation.

Professionals would previously use the term "ADHD types," but this is no longer relevant because presentations better show how your currently dominant symptoms can change over time. For instance, a boy can suffer from physical restlessness and no impulse control in his youth but start to struggle with anxiety, rumination, and internal hyperactivity later in life.

Common Challenges in ADHD Diagnosis

Unfortunately, even if you can meet most of the criteria, you can be denied an ADHD diagnosis due to structural barriers in the healthcare system and stigma from people with misguided and outdated beliefs.

Common reasons why someone with clear ADHD symptoms gets denied a diagnosis include the following:

1. Sexism: Ten years ago, ADHD was considered predominantly a male disorder. Hyperactive boys were by far the most diagnosed group and the most researched as a consequence. Since girls were taught to be polite, timid, and docile due to gender norms, their ADHD symptoms were masked and hidden, especially if they had an inattentive or mixed presentation.

2. Racism: Many marginalized groups and racial minorities are denied access to healthcare due to a lack of finances and money to spare. Furthermore, toxic stereotypes around laziness, impulsivity, and aggression lead many bigoted clinicians to dismiss genuine concerns about ADHD symptoms. Instead, they blame the individual and labels attached to their skin color instead of trying to understand the underlying cause for the challenges a person is going through.
3. Fear Mongering around Stimulants: With the rise of ADHD diagnosis comes an increase in the prescription of stimulants and medications. Unfortunately, many ordinary people and even clinicians falsely believe those stimulants are a cheat code taken by weak-willed and lazy people or dangerous substances that create harmful dependence and addiction. As a result, doctors try not to diagnose ADHD for fear of giving "junkies" access to drugs.
4. Wrong Diagnosis Due to Comorbidities: ADHD can significantly overlap with depression, bipolar, anxiety, OCD, and autism. If the symptoms of the other condition are more visible, you may receive a singular diagnosis, which doesn't show the full picture and makes treatment ineffective. For example, the inability to pay attention and stay motivated can make your work a living hell, which plunges you into a depressive episode. Still, the doctor only sees you are sad, low on energy, and full of pessimistic and hopeless thoughts.

Current Treatments and Therapies for ADHD

There is no one-size-fits-all treatment for ADHD.

Each person with the condition has a vastly different personality, list of strengths, lifestyle habits, environment, co-occurring mental health disorders, and bodily responses to various treatments. This is why personalizing treatment to the individual and trying out multiple options is always the best course of action. Here are the best options currently available:

Common Stimulants and Medications Used for the Treatment of ADHD:

1. Stimulant Medications: The two main brands are methylphenidate (Ritalin, Concerta, etc.) and amphetamine derivatives (e.g., Adderall, Vyvanse). They work by increasing the production of neurotransmitters, like dopamine and norepinephrine, to compensate for the impairments in brain chemical production and distribution. As a result, hyperactivity and physical restlessness can go down while mood, motivation, alertness, and focus tend to go up.[11]
2. Non-Stimulant Medications: This new type of drug includes atomoxetine (Strattera) and guanfacine (Intuniv). These drugs are also called selective norepinephrine reuptake inhibitors (SNRI) because non-stim medications increase the availability and effect of brain chemicals by improving receptor sensitivity. They can achieve similar effects to stimulants, but it will take longer for you to see benefits.[12]
3. Combined Medication Protocols: This personalized treatment plan involves multiple medications designed to

maximize the positive impact on ADHD symptoms while minimizing side effects. Combining medications under clinical supervision can help you achieve synergistic effects (stimulants increase the production of brain chemicals while non-stims enhance the sensitivity of the receptors) and create a more consistent symptom management effect (some medications result in instant effects while others boost your cognition gradually for a longer period).

Whether you decide to try medications or not depends entirely on you. Many people make the personal choice to avoid medications because they don't want to become dependent on them or the brands they've tried are not giving enough benefits relative to the side effects. They may also fear shortages and a lack of consistent access that will wreck their productivity and daily flow. Finally, some people simply can't afford them long-term or need to avoid using them altogether due to the chance of health complications due to pre-existing conditions.

If you do decide to try medications, remember the following:

- Don't expect sudden miracles. Medications make it easier to function, but they are not magical pills that will remove your ADHD symptoms.
- Medications can take some time to start working, and the side effects you may experience in the beginning (nausea, lack of appetite, sweating) will die down in the next few days or weeks.
- Try to stick to your recommended dose. If you have to increase because you do not see results, do it only after speaking with your psychiatrist, after waiting a few days to pass in the current dosage, and while staying below the maximum recommended intake.

Most Effective and Evidence-Based Behavioral Therapies for ADHD:

1. Cognitive-Behavioral Therapy (CBT): This is the most widely studied type of therapy, and it has shown promising results for ADHD patients. CBT is designed to help you change unhealthy thought patterns and the resulting harmful behaviors, like perfectionism that leads to overwork and burnout or low self-worth that causes people-pleasing, lack of self-care, and chronic anxiety and shame. It is a practical, goal-oriented, and structured therapy, so there is little ambiguity and confusion about what you should do.[13]
2. Mindfulness and Relaxation Therapy: Mindfulness is one of the newest therapeutic interventions. It is designed to make you more aware of your body, feelings, and thoughts while grounding you in the present. Slowing down and being present is the opposite of the ADHD experience, so many neurodivergent people struggle in the beginning. However, if you stick with mindfulness, it can help you manage your impulses better, focus on the present instead of overthinking, ruminating, and daydreaming, and slow down your usually hyperactive brain.[14]
3. Acceptance Commitment Therapy (ACT): This type of CBT focuses on simply being aware of your experiences without shaming and judging yourself. By fully accepting what you are going through without running away, you become less anxious and overwhelmed in the long run. ACT is an excellent choice for ADHD-ers with a recent diagnosis who struggle to embrace their neurodivergence fully. Just because you have an official diagnosis doesn't mean the doubts and imposter syndrome disappear. This is why ACT can be highly effective in gradually accepting

ADHD as a part of you and working with your brain instead of fighting against it.[15]

4. ADHD and Executive Functioning Coaching: Many ADHD-ers complain that conventional therapy is too neurotypical, especially if they stumble on the wrong therapist. ADHD coaching or executive functioning coaching can be a viable alternative because you will be working with someone who deeply understands ADHD and the unique challenges of neurodivergent people. It can be a perfect fit if you want practical solutions and suggestions for systems to manage ADHD symptoms better. (Warning: Keep in mind that coaching as a profession is unregulated by the government, so trying it is riskier because there is no guarantee about the actual qualifications of someone who calls themselves a coach.)

Most Popular Lifestyle Adjustments and Healthy Habits to Improve ADHD Symptoms:

1. Regular Physical Exercise: This can include everything from yoga to running. Physical exercise is the best natural way to increase your neurotransmitter levels, as it has been shown to enhance the production of dopamine and norepinephrine, which your ADHD brain doesn't have enough of. Make sure to do something you find interesting, enjoy, and can get steadily better at so that you are maximally engaged and not forcing yourself to work out. Otherwise, you are not likely to keep the habit long-term.[16]

2. Balanced Diet: Eating a wide variety of foods (fruits, vegetables, legumes, beans, whole grains, seafood, nuts, seeds, meat, and others) ensures you are not deficient in vitamins and minerals. This is essential because many

common deficiencies (lack of magnesium, iron, zinc, B12, omega 3s) can exacerbate ADHD symptoms. If you do any elimination diets (vegan, carnivore, keto, extended fasting, etc.), make sure to run it through a medical professional or a nutritionist so you avoid any nutrient deficiencies.[17]

3. Adequate Sleep: Sleeping less than six hours a day has been associated with ADHD-like symptoms (lack of impulse control, increased snacking, lower ability to focus, reduced emotional regulation, etc.) that will make your condition significantly worse. Long-term damage to your health aside, even a single night of inadequate sleep is enough to throw you off balance. If you are already vulnerable to disruptions in brain chemistry, stripping your body of the sleep it needs for recovery makes it even harder for your brain to catch up.[18]

UNPACKING THE ADHD MINDSET: HOW NEURODIVERGENT PEOPLE SEE THE WORLD DIFFERENTLY

If you have ADHD, how you think, experience your emotions, perceive the world and people around you, and navigate everyday life can be vastly different from a neurotypical person.

Inattention, impulse control, and hyperactivity take the spotlight for ADHD symptoms because they create common problems like procrastination, poor financial decisions, and chronic stress. However, the differences in your prefrontal cortex, neurotransmitter production and distribution, and other brain circuit alterations lead to a host of other often-overlooked ADHD symptoms. Still, you must know the full picture to truly understand how different your experience of an event may be from someone else's.

Underlooked ADHD Symptoms Related to the Perception and Processing of Experiences and Information Include:

1. Sensory Differences and Difficulties: People with ADHD may be more sensitive to certain sounds, lights, textures, or smells. This heightened sensitivity can easily lead to sensory overload, where you feel immense discomfort from some environmental trigger. You can also get overwhelmed by the sheer amount of sensory input you are getting since ADHD makes you less capable of filtering out and ignoring what your senses are picking up. This makes crowded environments, busy streets, or hectic workplaces a living nightmare for your ADHD symptoms.[19]
2. Differences in Time Perception: Have you ever been late for an appointment, forgotten about someone's birthday, lost track of time while obsessing over a project, or had no idea what day of the week it was? The changes to your prefrontal cortex lead to a cluster of symptoms called executive dysfunction, and one of the most common and problematic ones is time blindness. This means your ADHD brain finds it much harder to accurately keep track of time and estimate how much time a task will take.[20]
3. An Interest-Based Nervous System: Constantly pursuing different hobbies to capture the rush of novelty and changing jobs because you easily burn out and grow bored are two of the most sneaky signs of ADHD. Since your brain experiences disruptions in neurotransmitter function, you are more likely to feel understimulated and bored. If you can't naturally produce enough dopamine and other key brain chemicals, you start to crave highly stimulating activities (binge eating, video games, social media, passion projects, hobbies, etc). Essentially, you can be heavily driven based on what is interesting and engaging, not what is important and relevant to your long-term well-being.[21]

4. Rejection Sensitivity Dysphoria: Many ADHD clinicians report that a large number of their patients experience RSD, which is an immense feeling of rejection, sadness, and shame when receiving critique, constructive feedback, and suggestions on how to be better. Rejection sensitivity dysphoria can creep in even when you are talking with people close to you and even when the interaction has no signs of being negative and ill-intentioned. This intense shame or anxiety created by the anticipation of upcoming rejection can ruin relationships and make you more desperate to keep people by giving in to their needs without meeting yours.[22]

How People with ADHD Experience Emotions Differently

ADHD leads to issues with regulating various brain functions. Russell Barkley, one of the leading world experts on ADHD, has written multiple papers on how your brain differences lead to problems with self-control. This impaired self-regulation leads to inattention, impulsivity, forgetfulness, time blindness, and a host of other symptoms.[23]

It's easy to focus on those specific symptoms because they easily connect to problems with productivity and career growth. However, you don't just self-regulate your attention, motivation, and impulses. To be healthy and balanced, you also need to regulate and control your emotions. Struggling to do so leads to one of the most overlooked ADHD symptoms called emotional dysregulation.

Here is a list of some of the most common ways in which my emotions tune out of balance in everyday life:

- I want to sink to the ground with embarrassment when I make a silly and careless mistake.
- I get terribly depressed and melancholic for no obvious reasons and struggle to snap out.
- I have to hold back tears and breathe my way out of a breakdown when facing rejection.
- I get very upset and defensive when I receive critique, even if it's fair and constructive.
- I get terribly anxious and overwhelmed when I have multiple important tasks to do.
- I am drained and unmotivated most days, and doing boring tasks feels like torture.
- I feel my skin crawling and muscles tensing when I am in a messy environment.

Does any of the following sound like you?

For the longest time, I believed my personality and character deficits were the problem. I was simply too emotional and didn't care enough to control my feelings and reactions. This was until I discovered the emotional side of ADHD. According to Russell Barkley, ADHD also leads to issues in controlling your emotions, smoothly transitioning from one emotional state to another, and channeling your feelings in a productive direction.[24]

Everyone with ADHD has to deal with emotional dysregulation, but how it shows up can be vastly different. For some people, angry outbursts and crippling sadness after rejection is how it shows up most often. For others, growing unreasonably irritated while waiting or feeling overwhelmed whenever you have a lot on your plate is how it most frequently plays out.

Emotional dysregulation doesn't just affect how you feel or behave at a given moment.

Impairments in emotional control often lead to unhealthy coping mechanisms and lifestyle choices. For example, you can turn to people-pleasing to reduce the risk of facing critique and rejection, and you can increase your alcohol consumption to cope with your overwhelming emotions. Over time, those habits become second nature, and you start to mask and hide your episodes of emotional turbulence instead of addressing the root cause.

ADHD Strengths and Unique Advantages

While reading everything we covered so far is crucial to get the full picture of ADHD, listing symptom after symptom and problem after problem can be exhausting and demoralizing.

Instead, now we'll focus on some of the unique strengths that people with ADHD have compared to neurotypicals. At the same time, talking about those advantages as "superpowers" (a common phrase and narrative on social media) may be an exaggeration. It can't be denied that being neurodivergent has unique cognitive traits that can partially compensate for your symptoms and make life much more meaningful, diverse, and exciting.

Unique ADHD Strengths You Likely Have:

1. Hyperfocus Capability: You can't get started but can't stop once you do. If you have several hours to spare on something you find interesting, you will likely get hyperfocused, which is a cognitive state of deep immersion and concentration toward a single task. While many people with ADHD struggle with paying attention, daydreaming, and getting stuck in their heads instead of working, setting

up your environment and life to allow for hyper-focus can significantly increase your productivity.[25]

2. Creativity: Being creative is one's ability to connect different ideas, concepts, and thoughts in a unique way that produces something original, innovative, and useful. ADHD-ers are notorious for being out-of-the-box thinkers because they struggle to filter out information and ignore emotions and thoughts, which is challenging regarding their stress levels but highly effective in connecting different ideas, concepts, and thoughts. If the brain is a gigantic library and your prefrontal cortex can absorb information and sort it into the appropriate sections, having ADHD jumbles everything together with no sections. So, you constantly roller skate from one section to another instead of walking into strictly separated categories. Furthermore, being driven by curiosity and impulsivity means ADHD-ers are more prone to have a decent understanding of multiple fields, allowing them to naturally combine different fields and disciplines and come up with totally random suggestions that appear absurd at first but end up working.[26]

3. Spontaneity: Due to their natural impulsivity, people with ADHD are bolder, more spontaneous, and more willing to experiment. If you make more decisions on a whim and have an intense desire to follow thrill, novelty, and curiosity whenever they lead you, you are more likely to gather wisdom and new insights and become even more capable of creative solutions and problem-solving. This risk-taking and desire to constantly do something and initiate change is likely why such a large amount of entrepreneurs and business owners have strong ADHD symptoms.[27]

4. Passion: They say that passion, the ability to intensely and boldly express who you are and your feelings, makes you human and defines you as a living creature. Passion attracts people because it signals to others that you are not afraid to be honest and reveal your feelings. It's also contagious; being passionate inspires others to express their feelings. People with ADHD are naturally passionate since they only pursue projects that fully resonate with them, and they are not afraid to take the initiative and fully devote themselves in hyper-focus to what matters to them.
5. Empathy: Many people with ADHD, due to their strong and intense emotions, are naturally empathetic toward others. Furthermore, exposure to social challenges, conflicts, and heated situations due to your symptoms means you have greater social awareness and understanding of what others who struggle are going through, which is key for empathy. Finally, every moment you spend ruminating over your mistakes and anxiously thinking about how to self-regulate your behavior in fear of rejection contributes to a greater understanding of how many natural flaws, behavioral biases, and issues with self-control people have. If you have been down in the trenches, showing compassion to others in pain is much easier.
6. Resilience: Resilience is the ability to adapt, no matter the change in circumstances and what life throws in your way. A resilient person can overcome a harsh breakup, cope well with employment difficulties, and face life's hardships while coming out on top. Having ADHD is a lifetime exercise of accidentally starting fires and learning how to put them out effectively, and repeated exposure to challenges makes you more mentally tough and capable of dealing with the next problem that arises. When you live in

a neurotypical world that's not designed to accommodate and support your unique brain, it's only natural for you to learn coping mechanisms, strategies, and whole systems to survive and push through everything (especially if you have a late ADHD diagnosis).

The ADHD strengths you possess give you immense potential, but we shouldn't blindly glorify them without acknowledging the potential downsides and the context in which they have developed. For example, hyper-focusing on a start-up idea you are developing as a passion project is amazing. However, if you get glued to your screen for several hours while binging a whole session of a TV show, this would be a counter-productive and harmful way of using your hyper-focus abilities.

This is why setting up your environment, the headspace you are in before making a decision, and what you decide to channel your strengths toward are as important as the positives that come with your ADHD.

CHAPTER 2
THE CHAOS OF CLUTTER NAVIGATING ADHD'S ORGANIZATIONAL MINEFIELD

Overflowing kitchen sinks. Piles of clothes in every room. Laundry baskets stacked with dirty clothes. Items and toys scattered across the floor or shoved into a corner.

This is often the reality of your home when you have ADHD. Keeping clean sounds possible in theory, but something always goes terribly wrong along the way.

This chapter will help you turn cleaning, organizing, and decluttering from impossible to attainable and sustainable. To do that, we will focus on all the contributing factors that get in the way before giving personalized solutions to address each obstacle along the way.

UNDERSTAND THE CONNECTION BETWEEN CLUTTER AND ADHD

Many ADHD symptoms make it harder to keep up with home duties, leading to cluttered spaces that create visual discomfort and stop you from taking care of yourself.

Let's go through those symptoms one by one:

1. Impulsivity: ADHD causes impairments in impulse control, making it easier to give in to urges and cravings, even if they are not a good idea. This often leads to buying items you don't need, which you are then reluctant to throw away because you already invested so much. The more items you buy, the harder it becomes to keep everything together, and the more overwhelmed you are likely to feel.
2. Under-Stimulation: Brain chemical disruptions (dopamine, norepinephrine, etc.) make ADHD brains crave excitement, novelty, and variety. This can make it difficult to declutter and clean if you find it boring. Furthermore, shopping can give you a huge dopamine spike, increasing unnecessary spending. Finally, you may switch between hobbies more often, which means buying equipment and tools for each new special interest, which eventually adds up over time.
3. Emotional Dysregulation: ADHD can also make it hard to control your emotions and calm yourself down. This can lead to excessive judgments and feeling like a failure when you struggle to declutter. Furthermore, being deeply affected by events in your everyday life means the intense emotions prevent you from sitting down to keep your home clean because your head is elsewhere. Finally, if you get started, emotional dysregulation makes it easier to get overwhelmed and suffer from severe anxiety due to everything you have to do.
4. Working Memory Issues: Forgetfulness and impairments in short-term memory are some of the most common ADHD symptoms. They can make it significantly harder to stay organized because you often misplace items and

forget where you left them. This increases the time you need to collect everything and makes the decluttering process much more stressful.
5. Action Paralysis: This is another symptom of executive dysfunction, which makes starting tasks very hard. You can have everything prepared and feel ready, but you will be blocked by an invisible wall that stops you from taking the first step. Action paralysis is different from procrastination because you have no intention of delaying your tasks. Rather, your brain makes it harder to get started, as if you are caught in invisible chains that refuse to let go.
6. Unprocessed Trauma: ADHD makes everyday life harder, which can increase the chance for negative and traumatic experiences early in childhood. Many ADHD adults have unprocessed trauma from their childhood related to cleaning and decluttering. When such tasks bring out feelings of inadequacy, self-loathing, and shame, it can be difficult to get started because of the deep association.[1]

Unfortunately, the more clutter you have in your home, the bigger the harm to your mental health.

First, clutter can create sensory overload because more items are in sight. This can get worse if you are also bombarded with unpleasant smells that further contribute to feeling overwhelmed. The visual discomfort can turn into avoidance, making the problem worse.

Second, clutter can create negative thoughts and exacerbate overthinking and rumination. Many primary caregivers, parents, and people with roommates know the deep shame of not being on top of their cleaning duties, which makes them feel like they are an utter failure.

Finally, clutter and ADHD symptoms are deeply connected. When one gets worse, the other quickly follows. It's hard to sit down and work on your desk if your whole room is a mess and your desk is stacked with all sorts of items. The more clutter you have, the more distracted, anxious, and tense you will likely feel.

Let's break this vicious cycle.

UNTANGLING THE EMOTIONAL SIDE OF CLUTTER: ERASING SHAME BY FOCUSING ON FUNCTION OVER PERFECTION

Before diving into the practical advice, there are two key mindset changes you need to consider:

First, perfectionism is the enemy.

Keeping your home clean is as much about emotions as much as it is about having the right system. If thinking about cleaning instantly brings up dread and misery, no productivity hack can save you.

In theory, perfectionism can push you to try harder and do as much as possible. However, the high standards you set for yourself make it nearly impossible to feel like you've done enough. If you don't feel good as a result of your effort, you are much more likely to feel demoralized and unmotivated.

Furthermore, the higher your standards, the more pressure you feel to do well. This can be helpful if you are already working, but more often than not, perfectionism makes action paralysis even worse. If your brain gets stressed at all the pressure you put on yourself, the automatic reaction is to run away from the discomfort and avoid decluttering and cleaning as much as possible.

How do you defeat perfectionism?

Focus solely on functionality. The point of decluttering, organizing, and cleaning is to easily find what you are looking for and to have clean clothes, clean dishes ready for cooking, and enough space to work.

Having a few dishes in the sink is fine if you cook for yourself. Procrastinating on two laundry baskets stacked with clothes is okay if you have clean clothes to wear. Throwing out the trash tomorrow is not the end of the world if there is still space to fill.

Have you ever visited a friend's home only for them to profusely apologize over and over again for their place being a total mess? Then you look around, and it really isn't. The gentleness, kindness, and non-judgmental compassion we often have for loved ones is something we owe to ourselves as well.

Yes, your home would look even better if there was absolutely no clutter, every piece of clothing was clean, and all the dishes were polished and off the sink, but is this perfect state even desirable?

When you struggle with managing your ADHD, if something is worth doing, then it's also worth doing it halfway through. For instance, cleaning all the dishes at once would be perfect, but it's enough to clean what you need for the next meal if you are feeling low on energy.

The second mindset shift is that you don't have to associate your self-worth with the state of your home.

Many people automatically attribute moral failure (laziness, irresponsibility, and incompetence) to their character when they struggle to keep up with cleaning duties. This is not a surprise because in our childhood, our parents often:

- Give us tasks at home and punish us when we fall behind, which suggests that success in decluttering says something about our value as people
- Teach us that keeping your house perfectly clean is a sign of a responsible, disciplined, and organized person
- Feel the need to overcompensate by keeping everything perfect at home to make up for low socioeconomic status and other structural problems (poverty, racism, marginalization, etc.)

Our parents teach us about our worth as partners, parents, and human beings through various means. They might directly tell us, use coercion, or yell, or we might learn simply by observing their actions and words. From these interactions, we come to understand that our value in love, respect, and appreciation depends on the work we do at home.

If you step back, breathe deeply with a few slow exhales, and stare at this concept for a while, you will notice something: This notion doesn't make a lot of sense.

Your dirty clothes, stained dishes, and items spread on the floor don't speak. They don't judge you. They can't say whether you are a failure or not. It's your own voice, shaped by the toxic norms of other people, that makes the judgment.

Everything in your home is designed to serve you, but associating moral qualities (good and bad, competent and lazy) makes you a slave to your items. Instead of controlling them to make your life easier, they end up controlling you and turning your life into a living hell.

This cycle of shame and self-loathing has to stop on both sides. When we praise ourselves for finally being good people when we clean the whole apartment during one weekend, it allows us to judge ourselves for being bad people when we can't repeat this success the next weekend.

In one world, you see the overflowing kitchen sink, feel ashamed and guilty, look for every other task you are behind on, and get even more anxious and overwhelmed. On the other hand, you see the same kitchen sink, clean a few dishes so you can have breakfast, and decide to try cleaning more tomorrow when you have more energy.

Your home doesn't have a mouth. It can't judge you. It exists to serve you, so allow yourself a break and worry only about doing enough to function well. Everything else is a bonus.

It'd be nice for everything to go perfectly well, but you can live without it. When you struggle, it's not a sign of being a horrible and incompetent person. It's normal to have challenges keeping up with chores, especially when you have ADHD. When you feel at your worst, doing the bare minimum is an amazing achievement.

SETTING UP ADHD-FRIENDLY SYSTEMS TO PREVENT AND REDUCE CLUTTER

The right system will differ from person to person. Even if two people have ADHD, their most common and dominant symptoms, personality, preferences, schedule, and life circumstances can vastly differ.

There is only one universal rule: Work with your brain instead of against it.

Every piece of advice you will hear should be taken as a suggestion that you test out before making a final decision. There is no objectively optimal path you have to follow. The right system comes from deep introspection and extensive trial and error.

To speed up the process, here are a few helpful strategies and suggestions to consider:

1. Journal to Discover Intrinsic Motivation: Perfectionism, self-loathing, and shame are all uncomfortable to experience, but you may cling to them because they offer some motivation to work. You can free yourself only by reflecting on why you are doing a task and creating your own intrinsic motivation. For example, cleaning the kitchen allows you to cook and nourish yourself, gives you the space to prepare ingredients and meals in advance, keeps you free from bacterial infections, and allows you more variety in what you can cook on the spot. You can pick anything else you want and design your own motivation.
2. Find Your Rhythm Instead of Chasing Habits: The ADHD brain craves novelty and variety and experiences large differences in energy and motivation day-to-day, so habits can be hard to maintain. This is why doing a bit of cleaning every day may not work for you. If you naturally work best when you feel high in energy and hyper-focused on the task, it may be better to dedicate a few larger chunks of time throughout the week, especially the weekend. As long as the work gets done, it doesn't matter if your efforts don't follow a traditional schedule or set of habits.
3. Reduce Overwhelm by Focusing on the Essentials: Tidying up is not a single gigantic task but a series of multiple smaller steps. Among those smaller steps, some are much more important than others. Removing the trash from all rooms, putting dirty clothes into baskets for laundry, and using dishes and utensils in the sink are much more important than organizing your book collection. You need

to declutter as the biggest priority (remove trash and place items where they belong), next clean enough essential items to function (dishes, clothes, etc.), and then organize your belongings for work (keys, wallet, laptop, backpack, etc.). Everything else is optional when you find the time.

4. Do Tasks in an Enjoyable Way: This matters the most, even if it's not the most efficient way. Don't want to use a sponge and a cleaner for a quick swipe? Use wet wipes. Prefer to organize dirty dishes before putting them in the washing machine? Do it, even if it takes a bit more time. For everything you do, there is a way to spend the least amount of effort for the best results. However, if your brain doesn't enjoy the method, you will likely skip it altogether. Following what feels good is better for getting some work done, even if you are not maximally efficient.

5. Work with Your Brain's Intuition Instead of Against It: Do you have an intended place for your keys and wallet but keep placing them somewhere else? Well, maybe it's time to change your default placement to where it goes when you are not thinking. Your brain automatically makes choices based on what is most convenient and easiest. So, you can try to listen to it more instead of implementing someone else's system for everything.

6. Don't Be Afraid to Rely on Other People: If you have a roommate, partner, or children, there are ways you can outsource some of the labor to them. This is not only an option but a way to establish a healthy balance in the relationship. If you already rely on others, there are ways to use social pressure to get yourself to work. For example, you can invite friends and family over for dinner or simply hang out to create urgency to clean up the house.

7. Make Everything as Visible as Possible: Out of sight, out of mind is true with ADHD. Impairments in executive

function make it hard to remember something when you are not clearly seeing it. This is why you want to make everything as visible as possible. You can do that by relying more on stacking items in open spaces, like countertops and shelves. You can also use transparent boxes for storage, glass containers in the kitchen, or colorful labels with writing that indicate what a compartment contains.

8. **Multi-Task While Doing Your Chores:** This may be necessary if there is no easy, intuitive, or enjoyable way of doing something. You can turn on music and dance around while cleaning, watch a show on the side while taking care of the dishes, or listen to a podcast while sorting out the laundry. You can combine the social pressure we just talked about with multi-tasking by getting on a call with a friend to keep yourself occupied and engaged while working on the side. It is even better if they are also tidying up because it gives both of you motivation not to stop.

All those suggestions are designed as highly flexible rules, which allows you to customize your system in a way that works for you.

For example, some people put everything in boxes and compartments with colorful labels, while others prefer highly visible spaces, so they put everything on shelves. Similarly, one set of people will naturally start de-cluttering because they don't like how the situation looks, while another will need additional stimulation to make the experience more enjoyable and less overwhelming.

You can't go wrong as long as the system comes from you.

Minimalist Approaches Tailored for the ADHD Lifestyle

If only a single system could be suggested as compatible with ADHD, it'd be minimalism.

This is a quality (functionality) over quantity approach to your home design and possessions. Minimalism encourages you to have as few possessions as possible, which makes it easier to keep track of everything, reduces the need to move around the house to search for things constantly, and makes cleaning duties less burdensome. Furthermore, the significant reduction in items makes your living space less visibly overwhelming and reduces the anxiety and distractibility caused by crowded rooms.

Finally, de-cluttering under the principle of minimalism can give you significant momentum to throw away items you've been meaning to for a while. It allows you to re-frame purging possessions as a fresh start toward an entirely new aesthetic instead of throwing away items as a way of admitting you were wrong for buying them.

Minimalism isn't an all-or-nothing approach to life. It goes without saying that parents of young children who need lots of items to nurture and keep them occupied are primary caregivers, and people under specific circumstances can't reduce their possessions because they all serve a specific function. However, you can always try to take small steps toward a more minimalism-friendly environment.

Here are a few strategies you can try to reduce clutter through minimalism:

1. Make Each Item Go through a Questionnaire: Items and possessions remain if they have a strong practical purpose or significant personal value. The latter is highly

subjective, but for the first criterion, you can ask yourself the following questions: a) How is this item useful to me? b) How often do I use this item? c) Can this item's function be replaced by anything else to a sufficient degree?

2. Re-Assess Emotional Attachment to Items: We cling to a lot of items because we feel guilt for buying them (clinging to them can mean it wasn't a waste), we don't want to let go of the past, or they hold personal value to us (awards for achievements, given to us by someone important, bought when visiting another country, etc.). You don't have to throw away anything that brings you immense joy, but think twice about how much happiness each item brings you. Does the sentimental value of something justify the additional effort you put toward maintenance and cleaning and the potential overwhelm it can cause on top of everything else? If not, it may be time to go.

3. Set a Quota for the Removal of Items: A quota simply means the total amount of items you want to throw away. If you are dealing with significant clutter, junk, and other useless items, you can set it as high as 50 percent. For most people, setting a 2:1 rule (throwing away one item for every two items you keep) should be enough to remove many items effectively without much doubt. You can keep a similar version of the rule even after you are done purging through your rooms. For example, some people have a 1:1 rule for new items, making it mandatory to throw away something if they want to get a new item. You don't have to be as strict, but it's useful to think long-term in a way that prevents clutter from accumulating after you deal with it.

4. Introduce Waiting Periods for Current Possessions: You won't reach a clear answer for many items you evaluate. This is why you can take a few boxes and put all the items

you are uncertain about. Give it six to 12 months, and check on the items again. If you haven't used them once, it's time to throw them away unless they have a specific function for emergencies. If you used them in this timespan, ask yourself how often it happened.

5. Introduce Waiting Periods for Items You Want to Buy: The point of minimalism isn't to become a Zen monk with no possessions but to increase the requirements for functionality for each new item you get. If you want to buy something, it needs to fight for its life to justify if it's needed. If you feel an impulse to buy something, compromise with your brain by promising yourself that you will save for it and get it in three months if you still feel strongly about it. More often than not, you will have completely forgotten about it, or it will not seem as essential as it seemed back then when you initially felt the impulse to make a purchase.

HOW TO COPE WITH PROCRASTINATION: STRATEGIES TO OVERCOME PROCRASTINATION AND ACTION PARALYSIS

The final and most common obstacle ADHD-ers experience with de-cluttering is action paralysis. You can have the perfect system prepared, but you just can't get your brain to click the start button.

Here are a few ways you can make the beginning easier:

1. Slow Down Your Body: It's hard for your mind to switch between phone scrolling on the couch to clean dirty dishes in the kitchen sink. Your mind is hyperactive like an engine going 200 mph, and you are used to getting immediate rewards from whatever you have been distracting yourself with until now. To reset your system,

try a few breathing techniques that reduce hyperactivity. Two examples include the 4:6:7 breathing method with a four-second inhale, six-second pause, and seven-second exhale, and the intentional sigh, where you do a double inhale quickly and exhale as slowly as possible. Do this for 10 to 15 repetitions and see if you can get up then.
2. Use the Five-Second Rule: Action paralysis is often exacerbated by time blindness (the inability to assess how much time you have accurately). If there is no urgency, you can put off the task forever. One simple way to create urgency is to use the five-second rule, where you simply start counting from five to one and then immediately jump and get up. It works surprisingly well because we are used to responding immediately when time is running low in multiple other settings. Furthermore, the countdown creates the illusion that you have no other choice. The more you practice this rule, the more automatic it becomes, which is why implementing it in other areas of your life, like when working out, can make it easier to stick to the countdown when trying to clean.
3. Try the Pomodoro Technique: This is another way to take advantage of urgency. All you have to do is set a timer for 25 to 40 minutes and take a break between five to 20 minutes, depending on how much you work. There are even free apps you can download that automatically follow this protocol. The Pomodoro technique is excellent because you can see the time running out, creating pressure to get started. An underlooked aspect of the technique is the break you need to take. It's useful because the break alarm may ring off during your work. This is actually a benefit because interrupting yourself gives you even more motivation to continue after the break.

4. Start Easy and Small: Sometimes, even jumping out of the couch will be too much. But you can put your phone on the table, move one leg, then another, and get yourself up. If breaking it down to one leg at a time is not enough, break it down into even smaller steps. Shift your leg, slide it slightly to the side, and then move it ever so slightly repeatedly until it falls off the couch. The less effort you need to do initially, the easier it becomes for you to take action. The same principle applies to whatever task you have decided to do. Doing the laundry can start with putting five dirty clothes into a basket and taking a two-minute break, then another 10, then the rest, etc. You don't have to be a turtle throughout the whole process—only in the beginning. Think of it as an opportunity for your body and mind to warm up to the task. Furthermore, breaking the tasks means you can get a sense of accomplishment more quickly, which is an excellent way to pick up momentum.

5. The Five-Minute Rule: This is useful in cases where your action paralysis doesn't come from executive dysfunction. You can get up and do the task, but you don't feel like doing it at the moment. All you have to do is set up a time for five minutes and do the task only for this small amount of time. Since the effort required is so absurdly low, it's hard to skip doing at least five minutes. However, this small period will often be enough to warm you up and get you started, which is excellent since task initiation with ADHD often works like a faulty light switch. It's hard to switch modes and get started, but once you do start, it's hard to stop. In the worst case, you decide that you don't want to do it even after the first five minutes. This five minutes of effort is still better than not doing anything, and you will feel less guilty because you at least tried.

Those strategies can help you overcome action paralysis, but before trying them, you need to ask yourself if doing work is necessary at the moment. If you need to do an essential task that you can't function without tomorrow, then go for it. However, if you need to push yourself to satisfy your inner critic and prove something to yourself, you may want to reconsider.

While you can technically force yourself to the limit, it may be wiser to allow yourself to wind down, get your mind off work and responsibilities, and do something fun. Constantly being stuck in "working mode," even if you are not doing anything, can be immensely exhausting because your body is in a chronic state of high stress and anxiety, anticipating work even if nothing is happening. Getting deep rest is not only enjoyable and relaxing, but it will also help you feel more energetic and motivated the next day.

CHAPTER 3
ROOM BY ROOM REBOOT CUSTOM ORGANIZING FOR EVERY SPACE

We just laid out the general principles you can apply to any cleaning, decluttering, and organizing task in your home. It's time to get into the nitty-gritty of using those rules and other room-specific strategies to get your home in top condition.

In this chapter, you will learn how to create intuitive and sustainable systems that keep your kitchen, living room, bedroom, and bathroom clean and clutter-free.

KITCHEN COMMAND CENTER: COOKING UP ORDER

Keeping your kitchen in order should be one of your biggest priorities because your meals give you the energy and mental sharpness required for all your other tasks.

Creating a command center doesn't mean your countertop is always polished until it is shining and there is no speck of dust to be seen anywhere. It's enough to quickly make meals that nourish you and the people you live with daily. Your kitchen should be serving you instead of you becoming a slave to the kitchen sink, oven, fridge, and whatever other tool can be marginally cleaner and more organized.

To make your kitchen system ADHD-friendly, make sure it meets a few criteria.

First, your system should be intuitive. Even without thinking, you should be able to find the tools you need and navigate effortlessly. Second, you should enjoy being in the area. Even if there can be a marginally more efficient way, the more enjoyable it is, the less likely you are to avoid it. Finally, executive function demands should be minimal to ensure you don't unnecessarily struggle with action paralysis, procrastination, overwhelm, and anxiety.

Here are a few strategies that take those rules of thumb into account:

1. Considering Grouping Items Based on The Zone Where They Belong: If each part of your kitchen is strictly associated with a certain activity, there is no confusion about what you should be doing, and it is easier to keep working without losing momentum. To make the zones more efficient, you can place all relevant items as closely to the zone as possible. For example, utensils, pots, and pans can be hung on hooks near the stove to create quick access, and cutting boards, knives, mixing bowls, herbs, spices, and seasonings can be near the countertop or any other place you use for preparation. The same principle applies when you organize them across dividers in shelves. If you have anything in a container, make sure to use labels like "rice," "quinoa," and "flour" to make them easily recognizable.
2. Organize Items Based on What You Use Most Often: The first step is placing items in the pantry according to the

zone where they belong, like dry goods, canned items, and other staples with a long shelf life. The second step is organizing each zone according to how frequently useful each item is. Just like minimalism suggests throwing away items we don't use often, you can stash and put further back items that you don't use as often. In the example of the pantry, rice, flour, pasta, beans, and canned tomatoes should be further upfront simply because you are much more likely to frequently need them compared to seasonal ingredients or supplies for specific recipes. In your kitchen, you can try using lazy Susans instead of storing items (herbs, spices, seasonings, rice, flour, soups, etc.) in your cupboard so you can simply rotate and find what you are looking for instead of going mad while searching for the garlic powder.

3. What's Pretty Isn't Always Functional: We previously talked about how minimalism can be beneficial to reducing overwhelm and the choices you need to make. However, this isn't always the case in the kitchen. For instance, what's the difference between an aesthetically pleasing countertop with only three items and a stacked countertop? One definitely looks more pretty, but it's far from functional because you need to reach out to shelves to pick up countless utensils, tools, and other items. You shouldn't be ashamed of having a "cluttered" space because most recipes require navigating dozens of steps and ingredients.

4. Find Out Your Style for Cleaning: There are different styles of cleaning and de-cluttering in the kitchen, and there's nothing wrong with each style. Finding yours will save you unnecessary shame and frustration. For instance, some people can look at a pile of dishes and commit to cleaning only a few, while others can't get started unless

they finish everything at once. Your style of cleaning will also depend on your current mood. Some days, as the kitchen gets progressively messier while you cook, you may find the time and energy to clean the tools, utensils, and other items you've used while waiting for the meat in the oven to cook. By the time you have dinner, much of the work you had to do afterward may have been completed. However, not all days are like this. At times when you struggle to find the motivation to cook anything at all, it's perfectly normal to do the bare minimum by cooking your meal, putting the dishes in the sink, and leaving the rest later into the day or even for tomorrow. Not every day will be, or has to be, ideal.

CREATING HEALTHY, SUSTAINABLE, AND ADHD-FRIENDLY COOKING AND MEAL-PREPPING ROUTINES

Now that we have covered the basics of organizing and cleaning your kitchen, it's time to spotlight the main act—meal prepping and cooking. Before dicing into the practical solutions, it's necessary to briefly discuss how you can create a healthier relationship with food and cooking.

First, snacking, junk food, and "unhealthy" foods are okay in moderation.

It's universally accepted that non-organic, ultra-processed foods are not good for you. They can also exacerbate your ADHD symptoms.[1]

However, shaming yourself into abstinence will not lead to the desired result. Complete avoidance may be possible if your life is going well, but snacking is okay if you had a crappy day or when you just want to eat something quick and enjoyable and have no energy to lift a finger. Being healthy and snacking are not mutually exclusive.

For example, you can try the 80/20 rule, which allows you to allow yourself guilt-free cheat meals and snacking if the majority of your diet is healthy. Even if your eating habits can be more perfect and optimized, you need to consider what realistically happens when you turn toward the extreme. Your cravings don't just disappear, right? Instead, they build up and eventually explode in the form of binge episodes where you eat much more than any controlled snacking combined.

Second, the best diet is the one you will stick with.

How many times have you tried the latest diet trend, only to drop it in less than a month?

Diets may be medically necessary if you suffer from a chronic condition (obesity, diabetes, food allergies, high blood pressure, Celiac disease, etc.). However, in most cases, you are better off being in a low caloric deficit while eating a wide variety of natural foods (fruits, veggies, beans, legumes, nuts, seeds, fish, meat) and moving throughout the day. Sustainability is key, which is why healthy eating is a lifestyle, not a temporary band-aid.

Diets not only create a yo-yo effect (you eventually rebound and get the weight back), but the excessive restriction crashes your mental energy and motivation, making your ADHD symptoms worse. This is easily explained by the fact that the neurotransmitters you already struggle with (dopamine, norepinephrine, etc.) need amino acids (protein), vitamins, minerals, and omega-3s to be built. So, if you are not getting the building blocks and fuel, your attention span, impulse control, and drive will worsen.[2]

Perfectionism in the form of denying ourselves any "unhealthy" foods and extreme dieting are both driven by shame, guilt, and self-loathing. Just like with organizing, cleaning, and de-cluttering, there is no need to be perfect. Furthermore, what you eat in general and how often you eat specific foods doesn't say anything about your worth as a person.

Even if you are worried that you have to cling to the shame to feel motivation, know that the chronic anxiety and episodes of overwhelming emotions actually make it more likely for you to indulge in emotional eating as a short-term coping mechanism. You can always find personal and meaningful reasons to intrinsically motivate yourself by looking within. For example, wishing to feel energetic throughout the day and stay healthy to care for yourself and those around you are all amazing shame-free reasons.

The second aspect of cooking and meal prepping is designing the systems around the process itself. Here are a few suggestions to consider:

1. Pick Your Recipes Carefully: What's the difference between beef Wellington and spaghetti bolognese, smoked ribs and stir fry, lamb shanks, and chicken curry? The first takes significant time to prepare due to the dozens of steps and prior preparation required. The latter take way less time and are much more cost-efficient because you get more portions at the end. There's nothing wrong with wanting to cook something fancy if you can afford it and have the time. You can see a YouTube video for a stunning recipe and feel a strong desire to recreate it, that's great. However, unless you are passionate about cooking, most days, it's better to stick with recipes that give you more bang for your buck.
2. Balance Variety with Familiarity: If you are constantly cooking new recipes, you will always be overwhelmed, make mistakes since you are in the beginner stage, and

may eventually develop an avoidance of cooking. Similarly, if you are always eating the same food, you may grow tired of it and develop an avoidance of cooking or cravings for snacks and unhealthy alternatives in excessive amounts. The trick is to have 10 to 15 recipes in rotation. This way, you will have a set of dishes you can automatically cook without much issue (after practicing a few times), and you will have enough variety to not worry about getting too bored with any single meal in your arsenal.

3. Prepare Options for All Situations: Motivation and energy levels can wildly fluctuate when you have ADHD. Some days, you can conquer the world and smash through your to-do list, while other days, you struggle to do the bare minimum. That's perfectly normal, but it shouldn't lead to skipping meals because you are too overwhelmed and exhausted to cook anything. This is why you can have different recipes and options depending on your energy. For example, preparing yourself sandwiches, throwing a few vegetables into the air frier with some basic seasoning, making yourself an oatmeal cup with nuts, seeds, and frozen fruits, or a protein shake are quick options you can assemble in five to 10 minutes.

4. Don't Be Ashamed of Eating Unusual Food Combinations: Have you ever eaten cottage cheese with an apple, sliced deli meats, and two handfuls of walnuts? Maybe not this exact combination, but you probably have many meals that feel like snacking on many separate ingredients instead of cooking something. That's perfectly normal. It's okay if your plate doesn't look like the stock image of a regular lunch or dinner. Food is food. In all cases, eating something is better than not eating anything and starving

yourself. The less shame you feel about your eating habits, the less likely you are to skip meals.

5. Reduce Executive Function Demands during the Cooking Process: Cooking is not just cooking. Making a meal involves dozens of steps you must balance and often do together. It's easy to get overwhelmed, and the worse you feel while cooking, the more you want to avoid such unpleasant experiences in the future. First, gather all the necessary tools and ingredients before you start cooking so you don't have to go back searching. Second, take care of all the preparation steps for your ingredients, like seasoning the meat, cutting the vegetables, etc. Third, rely on written recipes, in-depth articles, cooking books, or professional apps unless you know the recipe by heart. Clear instructions go a long way to make the process less overwhelming because they reassure you how it will come together if you take it one step at a time.

6. Optimize How You Do Grocery Shopping: Optimizing shopping simply means creating a system that minimizes wasteful spending and reduces the chance of forgetting to buy key ingredients you need. You can create a digital note or chart on Google Docs, Google Sheets, or any other note-taking app. All you have to do is list all your commonly used ingredients, like eggs, sweet potatoes, rice, canned beans, etc. Next to each item, give it the status of "Have enough" or "Running low." Now, when you go shopping, you can list all the foods you will run out of soon. The list reduces the chance of forgetting something and helps you avoid overspending in the shop.

LIVING ROOM OASIS: DECLUTTERING FOR LEISURE

It's hard, if not impossible, to relax in your living room if you see a mess everywhere you turn. The clutter is unpleasant to the eye and can disturb you emotionally.

For a long time, my living room looked like it had survived a Category Three hurricane. Seeing boxes on the ground and clothes stacked on chairs made me feel lazy and irresponsible. Once those negative thoughts started spinning, I couldn't watch TV in peace because I felt a growing feeling of shame, guilt, and self-loathing.

If you have ever felt in a similar way, don't lose hope. Changing your living room and keeping it clean and organized can feel impossible now, but with the step-by-step approach I have described below, change is achievable and sustainable.

Transforming Your Living Room by Identifying Clutter

The first step in cleaning up your living room is identifying what actually counts as clutter.

The easiest way is to slowly scan the room with your vision and check for your emotional response. If you look at something and it brings up stress, anxiety, unpleasant memories, and associations, it's time for it to go. The opposite is also true. If you look at something and get sentimental, it usually means it can stay because it makes you feel good or brings back pleasant memories.

The first time I was decluttering my room, I even removed pieces of furniture, sentimental gifts from previous partners, and countless trinkets from my travels because they brought back stressful memories. Even if the ick you get from an item feels small when you look at it, remember that you have to be around this item every single day.

Checking up on your emotions can be an excellent way to sort out some of your items and belongings, but it doesn't always work. I assume you will have many cases where you don't have any strong feelings for a piece of furniture or an item on the table.

This is where you can start to evaluate items based on functionality by asking yourself some of the following questions:

- Does it serve a specific function?
- Does it align with your current lifestyle and goals?
- Does it enhance your life in any way and fulfill your needs?
- Would you bother to replace it if it gets broken?
- Do you use it enough to justify having it around?
- Are there other items already taking up the same or similar functions?

Using those questions, I threw out, put for sale, or moved to another room a lot of unused and old electronics, workout equipment (yoga mats, kettlebells, resistance bands, and dumbbells), and clothes that were stacked all over the room on the couches and chairs. Some were completely useless. Others could be helpful, but they were not useful enough to justify cluttering my living room.

Storage Solutions for Living Room Essentials

Even after thoroughly cleansing every possible source of clutter, your room can still feel too overwhelmingly crowded. To avoid sacrificing functionality, you can rely on various storage methods to keep the same number of items in your room without the visual headache and sensory overload.

Here are some of the easiest storage solutions to implement:

1. Pick Furniture with Hidden Storage Compartments: These can be ottomans with hidden storage spaces, coffee tables with lift-top mechanisms, storage benches, or any other piece of furniture that fits the aesthetics of your room while providing the opportunity to neatly hold onto many items in a hidden, or organized way.
2. Make the Most Out of Vertical Space: The most common options are floating shelves, wall-mounted cabinets, bookshelves, and vertical cabinetry. The furniture expands upward, allowing you to put a significant amount of items relative to the space you are taking in the room.
3. Use Small Bins and Decorative Baskets in Free Spaces: Those are great when you need a dedicated compact storage space for a set of items that don't quite fit anywhere, like remote control, small electronic devices, board games, puzzles, games, and media, children's toys, extra cushions, and throw pillows.

How extreme you go depends entirely on your style, how much space you have, and your budget. If you don't have space for much furniture, you can primarily rely on long horizontal cabinets and shelves. Similarly, if you are operating with a minimal budget, moving essential items to other rooms or relying on cheap alternatives, like storage boxes stacked on top of one another, is also a viable option.

BEDROOM BLISS: CRAFTING CALM IN PRIVATE QUARTERS

Keeping your bedroom in order is crucial to ensure you get the rest your body and mind need to function optimally.

High amounts of clutter in your bedroom can make you feel suffocated and overwhelmed, making it much harder to relax. Furthermore, having items from other rooms in your bedroom and doing many activities where you are supposed to be sleeping can make it harder for your brain to associate space with rest.

If your bedroom is messy and you don't know where to begin, you can start with the one-zone-at-a-time strategy. All you have to do is clear up one part of the room, place the items that don't belong in the bedroom in the room where they belong, and place the rest on the ground or on the bed. Complete removal is necessary because you are not only de-cluttering and cleaning but also re-assessing what items really have to stay. This evaluation can be done best with a clean slate.

Slow down by exhaling much longer and slower than your inhales for a few breaths, and look at the space. What do you really need in there to make it functional?

Let's take the nightstand right next to your bed as an example. You will need the lamp to not rely on the bright ceiling lights at night, the alarm clock to avoid relying on your phone and losing time in the morning, the current book you are reading so you don't have excuses to skip reading, and your sleeping mask to block all light that comes up early in the morning. Anything else, like headphones, charging cables, toys, and notebooks, has to go.

You can follow the same strategy for every other zone in your room, and eventually, you will get the space clean and organized.

Don't worry about doing everything at once, one additional benefit of taking it one zone at a time is that you can get results and feel a sense of accomplishment much sooner. If you feel exhausted, take a short break or resume the next day.

Keep in mind that the process of de-cluttering a room is a temporary solution. Alongside your current effort, you also want to ensure that you have a system designed to reduce the clutter that accumulates long-term. Here are a few suggestions to get you started:

- Use drawer dividers to store different types of clothes and have stickers with labels to make navigation easier.
- Store off-season clothing and special occasions dresses in separate sections and boxes, so your dresser has the clothes you need the most on top.
- Consider using wall-mounted shelves, organizers, racks, and hooks to maximize the number of clothes and items you can visibly see without taking too much space.
- Remove all decorative items and put them in another room, then slowly reintroduce them one by one so you force yourself to pick the most important ones and more clearly draw the line between meaningful addition and unnecessary clutter.

Finally, if you want to experiment with the minimalistic aesthetic we talked about in the previous chapter, the bedroom is the best place to give it a shot. Since you will be relaxing, resting, and sleeping in the room, there aren't many tasks that require specific tools and equipment. Since functionality is low, you can try to remove as many items as possible and see if you feel any meaningful difference.

An example of using minimalism in your bedroom is transforming your clothing system with a capsule wardrobe. This is a system where you significantly reduce how many clothes you wear every day by relying on different combinations with the same clothes instead of endlessly buying new dresses.

Here are a few quick steps you can try to make your capsule wardrobe:

1. Define the style that you want to have with your minimalist look. For instance, black, white, and red are commonly combined for a classy and elegant look, while pale green and blue, shades of gray, and white represent the modern minimalist look.
2. Go through your current wardrobe and assess which clothes fit the criteria. Since you are likely buying based on your preferences already, many clothes will fit the criteria. You can put the outliers aside for the time being. Separate the clothes you picked out into tops, bottoms, outerwear, dresses, accessories, or any other relevant category.
3. Choose the clothes that will be the foundation for your capsule wardrobe, like dark wash jeans, black dresses, white button-down shirts, and dark-tailored blazers. Foundational clothes are high-quality, durable, and fit in all or most dress combinations. Shopping for more if you don't have enough is perfectly okay because you won't need that many.
4. Look over the clothes you have prepared and start thinking of various combinations. To make it easier, you can take pictures of each combination and give it a label that creates context for when you want to be using it. You can create a folder with all the combinations and pick one

based on the occasion. This way, you significantly reduce clutter and decision paralysis because you instantly have a couple of outfit options prepared when you are hanging out with friends, going on a date with someone, or dressing up for an official event at work.

5. Consider throwing away, selling, donating, or giving away clothes that don't fit the capsule wardrobe's criteria. You don't have to go to the extreme when purging. If you have favorites that don't fit neatly into the concept, you should keep them. The same goes for seasonal clothes. For your capsule wardrobe concept, 80 percent of your combinations is more than enough.

Having a capsule wardrobe allows you to significantly cut the amount of clothes you are using, which reduces your laundry work and makes it easier to find what you are looking for in your dressers. Finally, the system makes you more mindful and careful with future purchases because you must consider how many combinations you can make from each clothing you buy.

BATHROOM SANCTUARY: STREAMLINING SELF-CARE

Bathroom decluttering and effective cleaning are all about finding the right furniture that will take up the least space while providing you with the most use.

First, anything above the floor is your best friend. This can include medicine cabinets under the sink for additional storage, adhesive hooks, or racks. You can store much more items while making cleaning substantially easier.

Second, look for furniture with a dual purpose, like toilet paper holders with storage toiletries, a shower caddy with storage shelves for hygiene products, and mirrored cabinets that can be opened to store items inside the shelves.

Finally, consider limiting the use of countertop space as much as possible. This makes cleaning easier because you have to store all items in the nearby cabinets and shelves. After all, if you don't have to move eight bottles and a dozen other items just to get started, you are more likely to quickly wipe through the surface before it gets repulsive.

Optimizing your bathroom with the right furniture makes cleaning easier, but this alone may not be enough. The cycle of failing to clean enough and then growing avoidant of the problem because you feel more uncomfortable is common in bathrooms because the rooms are usually smaller compared to other spaces, and this is where we are supposed to go to clean ourselves.

Many ADHD-ers find wet surfaces, sewage smells, and a host of other sensory experiences typical to bathrooms highly repulsive. This can create many problems, such as avoiding the bathroom as much as possible, leading to skipping hygiene habits, like washing your teeth or daily showering.

There are many easily implementable strategies you can try, including:

- Regularly use favorite scents, like citrus and lavender, to feel better while visiting and cleaning the bathroom.
- Steam clean the shower walls, glass doors, and nearby areas after showering to reduce soap stains and accumulation of dirt.
- Stock up on easily accessible microfiber and disinfectant wipes for easy cleaning or an electric scrubber to make cleaning in between your visits much easier.

- Buy strong multi-purpose cleaners that work for multiple surfaces (floor, countertop, mirror, etc.) to reduce the steps you need to take, like foam bathroom cleaners.
- Reduce sensory overload by using rubber gloves, wearing comfortable and non-restrictive clothes, and opening the windows and doors while deep cleaning.
- Try a soap dispensing dish brush attached to a hook in the shower so you can do quick scrubs while idle in the shower, like when waiting for your conditioner to sink in.
- Buy a high-quality shower cleaner, or make your own mixture with soap and white vinegar. Keep the bottle next to the shower so you don't forget, and use it once a week by applying the cleaner and quickly rinsing it off the next morning.

However, the biggest impact will come from consistently showing up and cleaning so you can avoid the spiral of feeling out of control once the clutter piles up to an overwhelming degree.

First, you want to set yourself multiple reminders so you can't physically ignore the need to clean your bathroom every week or every second week in the worst-case scenario. Second, you want to schedule a specific date, like starting at 11:30 am on Sunday, because simply writing down "during the weekend" gives you time to procrastinate until the last moment or not doing it at all. Make sure you have at least two to four hours to spare so you can't excuse yourself from starting by saying you don't have enough time.

Third, you can explicitly state to someone what you are going to do and ask them to keep you accountable, or at least mention it when talking with your partner, friends, and family so they can check up on you eventually. Fourth, you can try listening to a podcast, YouTube videos, or anything else that will give you the stimulation you need in the beginning. If you have a playlist of songs you associate with action mode, that's even better.

Finally, if cleaning your bathroom is your biggest priority, you may not want to start directly with it. This may seem counterintuitive, but cleaning your bathroom will likely be the most challenging part of the de-clutter and cleaning process because the sensory overload you feel makes it hard to be there for a long time. Trying to jump into the process out of nowhere may be too overwhelming, leading to total avoidance or severe procrastination. Instead, you can start with something easier, like cleaning the dishes, dusting off the countertops in your living room, and making up your bed before you move into the harder tasks.

Remember, just like with your bedroom, how you feel in your bathroom matters immensely. Functionality matters to avoid excessive clutter and reduce unnecessary spending, but how you feel is also important. We are not robots that merely want to optimize as much as possible, right?

I bet you don't want to feel suffocated, overwhelmed, and overloaded with unpleasant sensory input when doing your self-care rituals and hygiene routines. Not everyone has the privilege and opportunity, but changing your bathroom's design and structure through a makeover can be justified for better functionality, even if an urgent update isn't needed.

Sometimes, what bugs you in your bathroom will be something significant, like the colors or the ground, such as tile floors. Other times, it will be the little things, like specks of paint on the wrong surface as an accident during the previous paint job, the seams you have to clean and the uncomfortable caulk, or the laminate that feels much worse than the ceramic you want to replace it with.

It doesn't matter if it's the whole aesthetic or a tiny detail that stands out in an ugly and uncomfortable way. It makes sense to live with the discomfort of it if you are temporarily renting an apartment or staying somewhere for a few months. However, if you own the property and intend to stay for many more years, you shouldn't be afraid to renovate if you can afford it. Even if it's not the end of the world, the stress and sensory overload add up over time because you will use the room daily.

HELP OTHERS SIMPLIFY THEIR LIVES

"Clutter is not just the stuff on your floor – it's anything that stands between you and the life you want to be living."

PETER WALSH

In the introduction to this book, I spoke of the powerful connection between the tidiness of your home and your inner state. Researchers at DePaul University in Chicago have found that clutter negatively impacts your well-being, increasing levels of the stress hormone, cortisol, and making it very difficult to focus on tasks or relax in your home. For many, one of the worst things about disorganization is how powerless it can make you feel. The more things pile up in your home or your office desk, the worse you feel about yourself and the more likely procrastination is to take hold. And when you have ADHD, factors such as impulsivity, action paralysis, and unprocessed trauma can bring about negative feelings about yourself...feelings that stop you from moving forward and organizing your home or workspace.

I hope that by this stage in your reading adventure, you have seen that despite seeming like an insurmountable obstacle, clutter is, in fact, nothing. It is a collection of things you don't want or need. However, it takes introspection and an understanding of how the brain works to comprehend why we can often form such strong attachments to things that are stopping us from living in the sparkling, well-organized home we yearn for.

After reading about what clutter is and how it can take hold of you, you have jumped straight into a host of practical, easy strategies you can start from day one—including effecting a room-by-room reboot that can help you feel like you are living in a brand-new, gleaming, welcoming home you are happy to invite friends into. If you find that the tips you have read so far are enabling you to make strides on your path to a tidier home, please share your opinion with others seeking a solution just like this.

By leaving a review on Amazon, you'll let other readers with ADHD know that they can turn chaos into calm by following a small but highly effective list of steps.

Thanks for your support. Your words can inspire someone to not only tidy their home but also create a home that is inviting, comforting, and beautiful.

Scan the QR code below:

CHAPTER 4
DECLUTTER YOUR DESK, OPTIMIZE YOUR WORKING STATION TO REDUCE STRESS AND ENHANCE PRODUCTIVITY WITH ADHD-FRIENDLY PLANNING

If you work from home or in an office, the amount of work you can do from your desk will significantly shape the rest of your day. Your productivity not only pays the bills but also shapes your mood and determines the time and energy you have for other activities.

Getting your work done on time can be the difference between going home, cooking, and tidying up a bit before you sleep or staying late in the office. Similarly, it's hard to stay on top of decluttering and cleaning chores if you can't get yourself to start working in your home office and procrastinate the whole day.

Your environment can greatly influence your actions, which is why this chapter will teach you how to optimize your working station to stay on top of important tasks while minimizing resistance, distractability, and anxiety in the process.

CRAFTING YOUR ADHD-FRIENDLY WORKSPACE

The amount of freedom you have to optimize your work environment depends significantly on your workspace's environment, like whether you work remotely or in-person, and the willingness of your boss and higher-ups to provide you the autonomy and accommodations you need.

If possible, you can talk with your boss to make small tweaks in the work process to better support the way your ADHD symptoms play out in the office. These can include:

- Asking for written memos to avoid forgetting crucial details from meetings
- Getting clear deadlines and accountability checks by your manager, even if the project has no urgency right now
- Having a desk in the corner of your office space if you are prone to sensory overload
- Going for lunch at different times on different days so you don't interrupt your hyper-focus on projects
- Being allowed to listen to music or anything else that will keep you stimulated on your headphones without scrutiny

When discussing such strategies or anything else you come up with, it's important to emphasize that accommodations are mutually beneficial. You are not asking for "special treatment" but simply requesting more autonomy to create an environment that allows you to get as much work done as possible. It's a win-win for everyone.

This is what you can craft together as a team, but there is a lot more you can do. No matter if you work in-person or online, you can try the following strategies to enhance your working station:

1. Take Advantage of Context and Association: To make navigating the world easier, your brain creates labels for different places. If all you do is work on your desk, this is the default context. If working is the default association, it's much easier to get started once you sit down. You can strengthen this association by blocking all distracting apps from your browser and leaving all personal use to other devices outside your working station. For example, standing up to use your phone and drift off for a bit is okay as long as you do it away from your primary location for work (i.e., your desk). Distractions are inevitable and perfectly normal. All that matters is you eventually get back to work.
2. Remove Everything Non-Essential from Your Desk: Your brain also creates associations with the items you have on your desk. For example, seeing your phone reminds you of social media or the friends you meant to text. Furthermore, having many items on your desk creates anxiety and overwhelms you because you can't visually escape from the clutter while working. The easiest way to start over is by removing absolutely everything except your working device. Then, gradually reintroduce one item at a time, only if you need it nearby.
3. Keep Self-Care Items Nearby: One of the few exceptions to the previous tip is self-care items. For instance, having a water bottle nearby is crucial to staying hydrated, which is needed because dehydration directly leads to reduced attention, motivation, impulse control, and increased brain fog. Other common self-care items include stress balls, fidget spinners, grippers, and any other small item that can reduce spikes in anxiety and restlessness. Having them at your working station or nearby at arm's length is crucial because you want to minimize the effort required to get

them. The less effort you require, the more likely you are to use them consistently without getting distracted.[1]
4. Digitalize as Much as Possible: There will always be work-related documents you may need to print out. However, the vast majority of the paperwork on your workstation or around your working space should have a digital copy. This includes project memos, notes you have scribbled about current assignments and projects, and old business plans. When you have the time to spare, go through them one by one and ask yourself, "Is this relevant to my current work assignments?" If not, you can throw it away. Or, if it's useful, you can make a digital copy, write a short summary of the key pieces of information on a document, or file it away. You can also take proactive steps by requesting digital versions of all important business documents so you don't have to go through the organizational process over and over again.

THE UNIQUE CHALLENGES OF REMOTE WORK: HOW TO GET WORK DONE AT HOME

Those strategies are applicable for in-person and online settings. However, working from home presents a few unique challenges.

First, working with minimal distractions can be hard if you associate your whole apartment with relaxation and non-work-related activities. Second, you may struggle to get started due to the close proximity of many distractions, like equipment for your current hobby and special interest on the other side of the room. Finally, your 9/5 may not be stimulating or rewarding enough, so you need external motivation and accountability, which is harder to find when alone.

Let's address those challenges one by one.

The first challenge is associating your home with anything but work.

What you can do as a solution will depend on the amount of space you have in your home. If you live with other people or just by yourself in a single room, it may be better to find places outside of your apartment. This can be co-working spaces, cafes, libraries, and other places you can easily access reasonably nearby. Working outside is an excellent way to overcome the lack of external accountability because you feel pressure to get work done while surrounded by other people.

If your home has more space, you have more options. The easiest decision is to pick a place where you don't usually do anything like practicing a hobby or relaxing. Moving from your desk to the couch in the living room wouldn't work because you are likely used to chilling with the TV or playing video games there. However, working on the kitchen countertop while standing, seated on the terrace table, or moving your desk to the opposite part of the room are all excellent options.

The second challenge is nearby distractions. Here are a couple of strategies you can try:

1. Make Distractions Less Visible: You can take advantage of the golden ADHD rule "out of sight, out of mind" by removing anything you can impulsively distract yourself with. So, place any highly distracting items (phones, video game consoles, items associated with hobbies and special interests) into another room, or at least cover them up so they are not immediately visible when you are swinging on your chair. The same applies to digital distractions as well. You want to install apps and browser extensions that

outright block or create a time delay before you open YouTube, Instagram, TikTok, or Facebook. At the very least, you shouldn't have browser tabs of those apps open because you can constantly see them nearby and will eventually give in to the temptation.

2. Schedule Time Dedicated to Distractions: If you intend to work but have no clear idea when you will stop to take a break, your brain can easily go into panic mode. If the path ahead looks like endless torture with no relaxation, you get overwhelmed much more easily, leading to increased distractibility. When there is no clear separation between rest and work, you are stuck in the middle, trying to do both but ultimately failing at either. A simple solution is to make breaks mandatory, even if you are falling behind on work. You can take 15 minutes to guilt-free browse on your phone, watch an episode of your favorite show, or play with your pet. You won't see results immediately, but your brain will get used to the separation over time. A simple structure is 30 minutes of work with 15 minutes of rest, but you can adjust based on how exhausted you are and your work demands.

3. Warm up Your Brain before Working: Distraction serves a purpose, even if it's annoying to experience. When you feel overwhelmed, getting your attention off the challenging tasks helps you feel better, even for a few moments. Since context switching (suddenly jumping from relaxation to work) is a huge challenge with ADHD, you may need to put some effort toward making the transition period smoother. Like any physical workout, you want to warm up before you start the big tasks. This can look like going through your email and messages from co-workers and planning your goals for the work day before diving into the actual work. You can also take advantage of timers

again. For example, you can work only for five minutes and then rest for five, followed by working for 10 minutes and resting for five, and gradually build up your work time relative to the amount you rest. Don't underestimate baby steps.

4. Find Ways to Keep Yourself Stimulated: Immersing yourself fully and hyper-focusing on this month's huge project is great. However, you are not guaranteed to enjoy the everyday grind most of the time. When you are at home, there are a lot of ways to stimulate your brain while working. The easiest is to listen to music, but you can also turn on podcasts, YouTube videos, and TV shows. Just be careful, you want to stimulate yourself enough to be more alert and pay attention to your tasks, not get yourself hyper-stimulated and unable to focus at all. One way to keep yourself stimulated is to change your working environment from time to time. For example, working at your desk, dinner table, somewhere on the ground, or even going out to cafes and co-working spaces. As long as the environment occasionally changes and you can associate the place with work, you will be more alert and stimulated.

5. Check on Your Physical Well-Being: Your brain and body are deeply interconnected. So, check if you have recently drank any water, and aim for eight to 12 cups a day. Before starting work, have you consumed any food recently, preferably high in protein, so you feel satiated and give your brain plenty of amino acids to produce the brain chemicals you need? Movement is also essential. Throughout evolution, our brain first developed to execute complex movements in the savanna and eventually added the bonus of thinking, communicating, and doing mentally complex tasks. Your brain works optimally only if you are fairly physically active. So, when you start to feel

bored, restless, and suffocated, stand up and pace around for a bit. Even better, do a short workout with your body weight, dumbbells, kettlebells, and resistance bands. All you have to do is keep your body moving from time to time.[2]

The final challenge is a lack of sufficient external accountability.

Sometimes, when you must drag yourself to get the work done, the only reliable way is to have someone by your side. We already discussed how going outside, like in the nearby library or cafes, can create social pressure to work. However, this may be insufficient because you don't know the people around you, and it's not as if they are constantly checking up on you. This is why intentional scheduling with a close friend, family member, or coworker who also deals with a similar challenge can be immensely helpful.

It doesn't have to be a huge commitment. Accountability with a close person requires both of you to be on a video call and check up on how the work is done every 15 to 20 minutes or however long you feel suited to keep you going. The presence of someone on the other side may get you started. If that's not enough, getting reminders occasionally can be enough to snap you out of your trance and prevent you from drifting off as often in the future.

Finally, finding external accountability is important, but you may want to re-assess whether your current job is what you want to work. I am not saying you have to absolutely love what you are doing and turn your hobbies and special interests into a profession. However, you need to meet a minimum threshold of enjoyment for a job to avoid burnout and prevent yourself from struggling to the point where it hurts your performance and other aspects of your life.

It goes without saying that we take many jobs out of economic necessity, not because we want to torture ourselves for the fun of it. Furthermore, it's dangerous to give your two weeks' resignation and start chasing your dreams with barely any savings to your name.

Despite all of that, if you are unhappy with your current job and dread the end of the weekend, you may want to consider slowly transitioning and looking for opportunities elsewhere. You don't have to rush and take huge risks. For example, spending a few hours every weekend to develop skills for a different industry through courses and exercises or searching and applying for other jobs in your current field is a great middle ground.

Being content and engaged with your job matters because you can't optimize your way out of a toxic, suffocating, and mentally draining workplace.

DIGITAL DECLUTTER: MANAGING YOUR VIRTUAL WORKSPACE

Feeling overwhelmed due to the clutter in your digital spaces is one of the most neglected aspects of tidying up your working process.

It's easy to see how a messy desk can throw your concentration off, but it's harder to process the impact of the tiny but numerous distractions that slowly fragment and reduce your focus in the digital realm. Even if the impact of digital clutter is not immediate, it adds up over time and can eventually become a hidden productivity killer that tanks your performance when everything else is already optimized.

Here are a few strategies and suggestions to consider when starting your digital purge and declutter:

1. Assess the Usefulness of Each Digital Item Relative to the Cost: When we look at weekly newsletters, old links in bookmarks, and the hundreds of books in folders all across the desktop, it's easy to think of the potential benefit. At some unspecified point in the future, you may return to the article you bookmarked six months ago, or you may return to it in three years only to procrastinate it again. To assess the usefulness of anything digital, you can ask yourself how often you use it, whether it fulfills a unique purpose, and whether its existence justifies the overwhelm you feel. The last one is the most neglected because we think only of the potential benefit instead of comparing it with the rising sense of overwhelm you feel the more the clutter grows.
2. Create a System For Desktop File Organization: If your desktop is a mess, the time it would take to find something can discourage you from trying. The easy solution is to put everything in a couple of folders until your desktop is mostly empty. It will be visually pleasing, but finding anything you are looking for will be a gigantic headache. A better long-term solution is to make a folder for categories and characteristics that unite multiple files. For example, you can have an images folder in your "Personal" folder and break it down further by having different types of images in there. If you can't find an appropriate folder for something, it may be time to create a new folder.
3. Learn to De-Clutter Your Browser: Having ADHD means you have at least 20 browser tabs open at any time. So, here's a fun challenge. Close them all. Don't worry. This is not the end of the world. If you really need anything, you

will find it again. In the future, you should have a maximum of 10 browsers open unless you have a huge project or need to research something. More than that, it makes it harder to pay attention to individual tabs, which defeats the purpose of keeping them as reminders of what you have to do. Furthermore, the high amount of tabs is bound to cause anxiety because it creates the illusion that you are overwhelmed with work. Since executive dysfunction makes it hard to properly prioritize and put a label of "Important" and "Not important" on tasks, having countless tabs is bound to create paralysis. If anything is really important but you can't pay attention to it now, you can save it in a bookmark so it's not visually distracting.

4. Purge Your Email: Each email you get is a risk of snapping out from the task you had finally started working on after an hour of procrastination. Is the risk worth it? Probably not. The bare minimum is muting everything so you don't have notifications from emails bugging you. However, you will still get a visual pop-up or have to manually swim through the garbage sea of emails when you are looking for something important. Companies use lots of predatory tactics to get you on their email list, so occasionally unsubscribing, blocking, and muting common sources of emails is an excellent idea. When it comes to emails from newsletters, bloggers, and content creators, you have to ask yourself if the emails are nice to have or absolutely essential. If it's the first, it may be time to cut them out.

Less is more, especially in the digital realm. However, assessing what is truly important and clearly drawing the line between nice and essential can be hard. Distance not only makes the heart grow fonder, but it can also snap your brain back to reality and reset your judgment.

You can't just isolate yourself from the world and go live in a cave or a cabin for a month. However, you can take advantage of times when you are naturally off the clock, like being on vacation with your partner, family, or friends and during the holidays. The change in environment makes it easier to switch up your routine and avoid slipping into the habit of constantly checking your emails. Once you come back, you can more accurately see if you truly missed anything or what really matters to your working process.

Finally, digital minimalism should walk hand-by-hand with a reduction in how much you use your phone and other devices. Reducing your phone use greatly benefits your mental health, but it also helps you avoid overcrowding your digital systems with unnecessary content and tasks. After all, the more time you spend online and the sites you visit, the more spam emails you get, the more bookmarks you make, the more browser tabs you open, and the more cluttered your digital space becomes.

Using your phone is not the same as using highly addictive hard drugs, but reducing how much time you spend online is still a herculean task.

This is especially true when you have ADHD because impairments in impulse control make it easier to relapse and start mindlessly browsing. You have a recipe for disaster when you combine that with an ADHD brain's heightened need for stimulation, which social media instantly provides through cheap dopamine, and the tendency for action paralysis (once you start browsing, it's hard to stop).

Being chronically online can feel like a cage you can't escape from, no matter how hard you try. However, there are a few strategies that can tip the odds in your favor:

- Turn on focus mode on your device, block and delete apps from your phone, and install programs that create time delays before you can open specific apps. You can always break the system, but the added levels of inconvenience will often be enough.
- Find alternative ways to entertain yourself to compensate for the large dopamine gap that will form once you seriously start abstaining from social media. This can be through music, physical exercise, sports with friends, reading, picking up old and new hobbies, and anything else that seems fun and exciting.
- Learn more about your triggers by reflecting on how you felt and what you were doing before you started browsing again. This way, you can better understand what situations and emotions trigger your need to use the internet and social media so much and take measures in the future.
- Make it a challenge, either by competing with yourself or competing with someone else. Friendly competition can create lots of excitement and enhance motivation to keep going even when you want to break your streak of not browsing for hours. Doing it with someone else can also keep you accountable. If you are alone, you can try to increase the total time you spend without your phone each time to break your record.

Finally, remember that digital minimalism and reducing your use and dependence on digital devices is not an all-or-nothing game. Moving from 38 open tabs to 11 is a huge improvement. Reducing your social media time from 8 hours and 43 minutes to 3 hours and 11 minutes is astonishing progress.

Perfect can be the end goal, but good enough should be your current target.

HOW TO REACH YOUR GOALS ONE STEP AT A TIME BY CRAFTING AN ADHD-FRIENDLY PLANNER

All the steps we just described, as well as any other strategy in this book, will require some degree of planning where you track the individual steps you need to take and the progress you are making on them. Even if using planners is popular advice, especially for those with ADHD, it often receives exasperated glances and frustrated groans because hearing how you should plan your life to solve your problem quickly goes from interesting to annoying.

The problem isn't with planners themselves but with the burden we put on them. Expecting a new bullet journal or installing a new mobile planning app to turn your life around is unrealistic.

Let's go further and say it's probably unrealistic to think you will use it every day. Planners should be a tool in your toolbox of strategies—a system you heavily rely upon on specific days or certain periods but avoid using every day so as not to get suffocated and burned out.

Furthermore, the difference between a plain planner and a planner personalized for your unique ADHD needs is night and day.

Here are the golden rules to follow:

1. Make Sure You Can Customize It as Much as Possible: The planner must feel like it belongs to you. Otherwise, you will not feel comfortable using it. This is why you are likely to get the best results with bullet journals, blank notebook pages, digital documents with lots of room for customization like Google Sheets and Docs, or any mobile or desktop app with high design variability. Customization is key because the variety and novelty will keep your brain engaged. So, don't be afraid to make it as visual as possible

by making drawings, symbols, charts, and anything else that aligns with your creative vision.
2. Create a Clear Hierarchy to Establish Priority: What you find interesting to do will often clash with what's most pressing (urgent) or important for you. So, don't shy away from using numbers, pointing arrows, exclamation marks, and anything else necessary to clarify what you should do first. For even better results, you can have a separate list of the most urgent activities, so you don't even get to look at the other less pressing tasks for the day. Finally, if you are out of urgent tasks, you can grow more lenient and split it between one important task and something you find interesting to do. After all, the point is to balance what you need to do and what's exciting, not to ignore one side completely.
3. Adapt Your Planner Based on Your Success and Challenges: Do you struggle to complete the tasks you set for yourself and feel like a failure? Then, it's time to reduce the volume of daily tasks or make versions of your planner depending on your motivation and energy levels during the day. Do you write out all your plans only to forget about them? Then, set reminders and alarms to occasionally check up with your planner and see how much progress you've made. Many people give up on planners because they find them unsuitable for their workflow, but a better option would be to lower your expectations and promise to adjust your planner until it aligns with your vision.
4. Be Mindful of How You Are Setting up the Tasks and Actions in Your Planner: First, the tasks you put must have some sort of a deadline, even if you make it up. Otherwise, there isn't sufficient urgency to get you to do them. Second, you want to make the phrasing highly specific

with action verbs, like "Complete X, Review Y, Research Z." Third, break down tasks that are too big so it's easier to get started and pick up momentum once you finish a few small tasks. If you feel confused and paralyzed when looking at a task, it's either not specific enough or contains too many smaller tasks within it, making it harder to prioritize and know where to start.

Digital vs. Physical Planners: Choosing What Works for You

Choosing the right planner type can make all the difference depending on your style, needs, and preferences. So, let's comprehensively review what you should expect from digital and physical planners.

➕ Pros of Digital Planners:

1. Reduced Demand for Executive Function: Digital planners offer a lot of convenience because you can open an app and get started right away. Writing and updating your planner is quicker, which is neat if you are in a rush, and it more closely aligns with the natural high pace of the ADHD brain. Finally, you already have templates and an established structure in many apps, so you don't have to think much about design or can choose between a set number of options, making the creative process easier. If you struggle with getting started, digital planners are the superior option.
2. Long-Term Sustainability: If you use a dedicated app or know how to use Google Sheets and Excel formulas, you can track long-term progress and use statistics to see your productivity (overall performance). Furthermore, you can easily navigate between your current entry and planners for previous weeks, months, and even years. Finally, you

don't have to worry about the previous planners or the safety of your notes because all apps have digital backups.
3. Portability Across Devices: Many apps allow you to sync your to-do list and planner across multiple devices easily and even to automatically set up alarms and reminders so you don't forget about the task. Multi-device syncing is useful if you want to grab what's closest to you and quickly update your plan for the day.

— Cons of Digital Planners:

1. Association with Social Media and Internet Indulgence: Unless you have a whole device used only for your to-do list and planning, using your everyday electronic devices for planning can quickly turn into a gateway toward distraction. For example, since you associate your phone with social media and internet usage for a few hours every day, it's very easy to get tempted and respond to the impulse to get on YouTube, Facebook, Instagram, TikTok, or anywhere else instead of doing the work on your planner.
2. Payment Walls: Most high-quality planning apps will require some form of payment, like a subscription, to give you access to all their features. While you can stick with free versions, your options will likely be significantly limited. So, you have to be willing to accept the ongoing cost unless you decide to use free tools like Google Docs and Google Sheets.

+ Pros of Physical Planners:

1. Feels Natural: For many people, for reasons they can't quite explain, using a pen or a pencil on paper feels ten

times more natural than digital devices. Formulating their thoughts is easier, and they feel immersed and concentrated while writing. If something feels off with digital devices, the sensation may be a deal breaker. No matter the template, digital planners can't replace the hand-drawn designs, drawings, stickers, random doodles and symbols, and other decorative elements you can do.

2. Slowing Down Can Actually Be a Benefit: Digital planners offer more convenience and a quicker pace, but this comes with downsides. After all, when planning your day, you want to slow down, think carefully about what you want to include, and critically assess everything. Writing on paper naturally slows you down because your brain learns to adapt its pace based on your writing speed. Sure, in the beginning, you will feel some resistance, but over time, you will get used to planning in a slower and more thoughtful way.

3. Allows You to Associate Your Planner Solely with Work: Why is reading a physical book easier than downloading one on your phone? Well, every single minute, you are two clicks away from opening a much more entertaining and stimulating app. This logic applies to physical versus digital planners as well. If you buy a bullet journal, you are only using it to plan your days and weeks and nothing else. So, when you open it, you instantly get in the headspace for work, making it easier to get started and avoid distractions. Finally, having the planner right in front of you instantly reminds you of your to-do list that you need to update, but using an app on your laptop or phone doesn't always lead to the same effect if they are not right in front of you.

- **Cons of Physical Planners:**

  1. Tracking Becomes Harder If You Are Prone to Forgetfulness: You may forget the planning app is on your phone, but you will never forget your phone when going somewhere. The same can't be said for physical planners, like bullet journals. If you are in a rush or your mind is elsewhere, you can drift off while preparing your backpack and forget to bring your physical planner. Furthermore, physical planners rely solely on their visibility in your proximate environment, while many apps set automatic check-ups and reminders.
  2. Highly Painful for Perfectionists: Have you ever written a word in an ugly way in your journal and wanted to toss it out the window? The problem with physical planners is that you may not enjoy your handwriting very much, spend too much time trying to make your handwriting pretty instead of working, or get irritated when the whole page feels off and ugly after a mistake and revision. Comparatively, this problem doesn't exist with digital planners because the font is universally the same, and you can easily make corrections and revisions without ruining the structure and aesthetic look of the page.

As you can see, digital and physical planners have unique strengths and weaknesses. You shouldn't dismiss one unless you have experimented with it for at least a few weeks because this gives you enough time to try it out and work on personalizing it to meet your needs.

Furthermore, if you are hesitant to pick one over the other, maybe you can draw specific benefits from both. So, an alternative approach is to combine them for different categories of tasks.

For example, if your corporate job is highly dynamic and fast-paced, you can use a digital planner that you can quickly update and modify. You can use a physical planner to create a unique ritual around them for your personal goals, hobbies, and self-care habits that remain fairly static and consistent across several weeks and months.

Finally, you don't need to use your planner daily. Structure is a huge benefit in containing chaos and giving you a clear direction for what you should do. However, religiously relying on planners daily or pressuring yourself to always make a to-do list will eventually lead to burnout because you feel suffocated and excessively confined. It's better to use a planner three to four days a week for months at a time instead of forcing yourself to stick with it every day for three weeks before quitting.

CHAPTER 5
SOCIAL SYNC NAVIGATING ADHD IN YOUR SOCIAL SPHERE

When we think of our relationships with other people, the default assumption is to go with the flow. According to this notion, winging it will show whether you are naturally great at interacting with people or not. Furthermore, human connections are all about authenticity and genuine connection, so trying to optimize the way you handle social situations is robotic and unnatural.

Fortunately for all of us, such outdated beliefs couldn't be further from the truth.

Just like we apply a growth mindset to every other aspect of our lives, you can also significantly improve your social skills and how you manage your relationships if you prioritize and put conscious effort into becoming better. Reducing forgetfulness, articulating yourself more clearly, and getting better at planning your social engagements are endless ways to plan and design your social life to create new relationships and deepen your connections.

Getting better at engaging and connecting with people isn't fake and unnatural. It's actually the total opposite.

Going out of your way to better manage and navigate your social life shows that you deeply care about how you present yourself and how you treat the people around you. This is why this chapter will teach you everything you need to know to organize your way into a healthier, more meaningful, and more sustainable social life.

GETTING ORGANIZED AND PREPARING FOR SOCIAL ENGAGEMENTS

Have you ever seen someone's message and told yourself you would reply in five minutes, only to remember how you totally forgot two days later? Stopped talking with a long-distance friend for more than a month because you were swamped with work during that time? Forgotten a close friend's birthday and had to rush to get them a gift at the last moment?

Disorganization, time blindness, forgetfulness, and problems with working memory are all ADHD symptoms that can make maintaining friendships and other social bonds challenging. Struggling to show how much you care for people can lead to lots of guilt, shame, and self-loathing because it feels like you don't care enough, even though you know that you like, love, and respect the people around you.

Having ADHD can create a gap between your intentions and feelings toward a person and your day-to-day behavior toward them. This is why creating organizational solutions and systems to compensate for your ADHD symptoms is essential.

First, you want to create a system for scheduling and reminding yourself of upcoming social events. The simplest solution is the triple reminder calendar system, where you set up an alarm that will ring off a week, three days, and the day before an important social event. This should be enough to bring your attention, so you don't forget to prepare in advance.

You can also create reminders to push yourself to initiate social events, like getting a fixed reminder once a week to check up on your friends and ask them to schedule a time to catch up and hang out. When you schedule a meetup with friends, double-check if you have the correct information and add it to your calendar to automatically receive a notification. If you've got a ton of messages coming up, set yourself an alarm that will buzz and remind you to check up on all of them once you are available.

You won't always need it, but it's good to set up reminders just in case life gets in the way.

Second, you want to prepare in advance for social events. Unless you are constantly looking at a clock in your room, you are bound to lose track of time.

Since preparing in the last moment can often lead to you forgetting to get something important due to the stress of being in a rush, taking the time to prepare the outfit you will wear, your wallet or purse, and anything else you could need will be a huge advantage. You don't have to make a whole list, but if it's a social event that will last multiple days and you need to pack a lot, like going on a vacation, creating a list of items you need to get will be necessary. This way, you have a visual reminder of what you have packed already and what you still need to prepare.

Finally, even with the best planning in the world and items prepared in advance, you can still get unexpected delays at the last moment, like being stuck in traffic, having to go back because you have forgotten something, etc. This is why you can intentionally get into the agreed-upon location earlier than expected to be absolutely confident that you won't be late. Even if it's not absolutely necessary, it can be a huge relief that reduces your anxiety and rumination if you are there first.

All those strategies are relevant when you are going away from your home. However, you can bypass some of the obstacles in social events, like needing to be there on time and preparing specific items, by simply hosting gatherings in your home. This way, you can be in a sensory-friendly environment and don't need to commute back to your place after the gathering. Also, regularly bringing people over creates consistent motivation to keep your home clean, organized, and de-cluttered.

HOW TO NAVIGATE SENSORY OVERLOAD AND FEELINGS OF OVERWHELM IN SOCIAL SETTINGS

Sensory overload is a common but seriously underlooked ADHD symptom. It happens because you are much more aware of everything going on around you, seeing the vivid details you're an intensity that people may not be aware of. Not only is the intensity of what your eyes, ears, and nose pick up much higher than that of a neurotypical person, but you also struggle to filter out and ignore all the sensations you experience, leading to a painful cacophony in your mind.

At home, the uncomfortable texture of food, the itchy feeling of clothes against your skin, the nauseating smell of deodorants or shampoo in the shower, the subtle sound of your neighbors arguing on the other side of the wall, the never-ending humming of the refrigerator, or the blinding light from the window are all examples of subtle sensory overload.

Unfortunately, this feeling of drowning in the input of your senses can be even worse in social settings because the number of people, noises, and other sensory stressors is significantly higher.

You can't completely eliminate your discomfort, nor should you attempt to pretend you are not bothered. Still, you can take steps to manage the risk of sensory overload in social settings better.

Here are a few suggestions to get started:

1. Reflect and Learn More about Your Specific Triggers: If you are sensitive to your environment, there will be specific sounds, smells, and situations that bother you much more than others. In a physical notebook or digital document, take some time to write about times in the past when you felt overwhelmed and emotionally out of control. Ask yourself what was different about this situation compared to other social events and what had happened exactly that made those uncomfortable and painful feelings flare up. Regularly reflecting will allow you to spot patterns and recognize if you should be extra careful in certain settings, like loud nightclubs or crowded hangout spots.
2. Don't Be Afraid to Cancel or Re-Schedule Meetings If You Are Not Feeling It: Sometimes you will be more prone to sensory overload and have less control over your reactions. For example, if you feel yourself on edge and tense due to work-related problems, it may be better to avoid or just re-schedule a meeting with friends because you will be much more irritable and vulnerable. If you happen to be in painful periods in your life, you want to emphasize self-care, where you dedicate time to doing something that makes you feel cozy, relaxed, and comfortable instead of exposing yourself to additional triggers.
3. Communication with Friends and Family Is Essential: You are not alone, and you shouldn't be coping with sensory

overload and emotional dysregulation by yourself. I know it can make you feel needy, but you should absolutely inform the people you hang out with that you may be sensitive to certain sounds, smells, sights, and situations and that you may not want to participate in all activities or even want to go home early. This will allow the people around you to be more mindful of what they are suggesting as activities and will ensure that someone is checking up on you in case you are not feeling well. After all, it's sometimes easier for your friends to see if you are not feeling alright, and they spot it way before you become aware of the problem.

4. Prepare an Emergency Kit when You Are Not Feeling Well: There are many items you can take with you that can make certain social settings more bearable, like fidget toys, stress balls, chewing gum, or even noise-canceling headphones when you want to zone out for a few minutes. They are an excellent way to relieve stress and intentionally put your attention elsewhere, allowing you to ignore and stop processing what is happening in your environment. Relying on items will not be enough if the situation creates a lot of stress and discomfort. So, you shouldn't be afraid to step out for a breather occasionally or leave earlier altogether. After all, being out with other people is supposed to be enjoyable, not a prolonged torture session you need to endure due to social rules and conventions.

HOW TO RESHAPE SOCIAL CIRCLES AND CREATE MEANINGFUL ENGAGEMENTS

Having ADHD often leads to lots of unhealthy coping mechanisms that can hurt your social life in the long term.

For example, people-pleasing is common when you have ADHD since low self-worth makes you desperate for the approval of other people while simultaneously loathing potential criticism or rejection (rejection sensitivity). Similarly, perfectionism can give you the desire to never miss out on anything, convincing yourself that you should always do as much as possible.

Here are a few golden rules to keep in mind when shaping your social circles and engagement with other people:

1. Raise Your Standards for Friendships: Many people fall into the trap of remaining in social circles simply because it's convenient, and they fear they can't find better friends. Often, being with people can make you feel more alone and alienated than if you were to be by yourself. It's not okay to always be the one reaching out to others or constantly have to put out fires and set boundaries because the people around you refuse to give you basic decency. Especially when recognizing your ADHD, you should have friends who see you in good faith. When you make a mistake, they seek to understand without judgment instead of lashing out and trying to tear you apart. You shape your social environment, but it also shapes you, and a toxic set of friends can severely hurt your mood, confidence, and mental health.
2. Socializing Has to Be Balanced with Self-Care: Unless you are highly extroverted and genuinely feel energized after every interaction with people, you shouldn't accept every

possible social gathering and go just for the sake of being social. When you have ADHD, social events can be highly draining because you constantly need to self-regulate to avoid impulsively interrupting, drifting off and missing what someone has said, or over-reacting by reminding yourself that they didn't mean to offend or hurt you. Time alone with your thoughts and emotions is healthy and essential to recharge your social battery and have more mental energy for the selected gatherings you choose to attend. Finally, putting some distance between you and others allows you to more clearly see who you are actually missing.

3. Learning to Say "No" Is an Art You Should Learn: Many ADHD-ers naturally say yes to every possible social opportunity because of people-pleasing, social pressure, desire to be nice, or fear of what'd happen if they were to stand their ground. There are three ways to make it easier on yourself. First, say that you will think about it and get back to the person so you don't need to make an immediate commitment. Second, sit down and make a list of pros and cons. You don't have to write a whole essay, but a few points on each side is enough. It's hard to dispute an argument and reject an offer if you have it on paper. Soon enough, this pros and cons thinking will become your default, and you won't have to write down most decisions. Finally, offer rejections by being extra nice, explaining why you won't do it, and thanking them for the offer so you feel less bad.

Those rules are excellent ways to improve your decision-making when evaluating relationships and social opportunities. However, your philosophy on friendships and relationships in general is only one part of the whole puzzle. The last missing, and often neglected, piece is building up your social skills.

Many people with ADHD naturally struggle in day-to-day engagements and conversations with other people, and trying to get better feels impossible. Feeling discouraged is normal since building up your social skills can be much harder than many other tasks. After all, it's hard to quantify how much better you have gotten over time, whether or not you are progressing, and what goal you are trying to reach. Human interactions are so complex and overwhelming that it's tempting to throw down the gauntlet.

If you are willing to give it a shot, there are a few steps you can take to get started.

First, you need to accept that trying to be better will likely suck in the beginning. Patience is a virtue, especially when trying to get better at communicating with people. You will have times when you want to crawl back to your cave at home and never come out because you are unsure if you said the wrong thing, making you doubt your progress so far.

There won't be immediate results, especially since the skill you are practicing involves more than one person. When you go to the gym, try to lose a few pounds, improve your eating habits, and increase your sleep score, it's easily quantifiable, and you can see the baby steps and progress you are making. When talking with other people, you will get a natural high and deep sense of immersion when you strike the right balance in a conversation, but there will always be this creeping doubt, discomfort, and anxiety that makes you question whether you are getting better.

That's completely okay. The emotions you are going through are normal and human. Just because it feels uncomfortable and painful doesn't mean you need to take action, try to erase them, or escape from what you are going through.

Now, do not just read the next sentence and then forget about it.

Instead, write down a personal motto that encapsulates this message, like "I am slowly getting better, and it's okay for me to feel insecure and uncertain because that's part of the process." Don't copy and paste from somewhere else—come up with something original that resonates with you. Most importantly, repeat it as much as possible, say it out loud when you feel horrible, put it on stickers around your home, and bold it with a huge font in your digital documents. It will take time, but eventually, you will fully accept and embrace it.

Second, practice active observation of the person in front of you by understanding as much as possible about them through every conversation,

Conversations look simple, but every interaction requires you to understand what others are saying and accurately guess the intentions and emotions behind their words, facial features, body language, and other non-verbal cues. It's so complex that learning this skill will require you to break it down by focusing first on what the person is saying with words, and then as you get significantly better, trying to decipher more subtle cues, like what their tone of voice, body, and other conversation cues are suggesting.

All you have to do in the beginning is practice observing the other person and trying to understand them while interrupting them as little as possible. You are looking to understand their perspective on the topic you are talking about, as well as subtle or sudden shifts in their behavior while you are talking. By intentionally observing the other person, you get a clear purpose and specific goal, which makes it much easier to know what you are supposed to do.

For example, when you are setting a meeting with a friend, there's a difference between them beaming and expressing how much they'd love to go and are looking forward to it and them giving a polite smile and more passively saying that they are up for it as long as you are. If you see somebody's enthusiasm falter unexpectedly, you can look for clues about what happened or, if appropriate, ask them why they don't seem too excited about it.

While observation is a fine goal, it's still unclear whether you are successful in guessing what the other person is expressing, feeling, and thinking. This is why mirroring is such a powerful technique. When the other person is done talking, you want to start by briefly summarizing and putting in your own words what they have expressed, like "From what I understand, you are saying that..." You can always make educated guesses, but it's only through directly making a humble guess that you can confirm you understand what the other person is going through.

Finally, intentional observation and mirroring are an excellent way to understand if you have made a mistake during a conversation with someone.

No matter how much you try, you will inevitably drift off, zone out, miss and forget about important details, or impulsively interrupt the other person. It will still happen if you can reduce how often this happens. What's equally important is to use those observational skills and see if the other person gets more passive, distant, and withdrawn, which would be your cue to apologize and explain that you didn't make the mistake intentionally. This is not a perfect solution, but it's miles better than interrupting a person and rambling for minutes without getting the hint that they felt hurt for being silenced.

Third, you want to reflect on the most common ADHD symptoms that get in the way of a meaningful conversation and create a tool kit of solutions and strategies to implement in day-to-day interactions.

For example, zoning out and struggling to pay attention in a conversation for an extended time is a common ADHD struggle due to symptoms like inattention and distractibility. A few strategies you can implement include the following:

- Focus on the mouth or eyes of the person since it makes the interaction more personal and direct, making it harder to drift off.
- Count to five and take a few moments to intentionally absorb context clues about what's being discussed before speaking up.
- When you feel yourself spacing out, slow your breathing by extending your exhale to reduce your internal hyperactivity and ground yourself.
- Don't be afraid to tap your feet, play with your hair and the edges of your clothes, bounce in your seat, or even pace around the room if it helps you stay focused.
- Sometimes, you will zone out accidentally, so apologize quickly and gently ask for the information you have missed, like by saying, "I did hear you say that, but not the rest. Can you repeat that, please?"

Another common example of ADHD getting in the way of a balanced conversation is impulsivity, leading you to unnecessarily interrupt someone else when they are speaking or saying something inappropriate and out of place. Here are a few suggestions you can try:

- Count to five when a person stops speaking, and only after that say something yourself to make sure you are not interrupting them.
- Delay your immediate response to something by coming up with phrases like "That's interesting" and "Let me think about that" to give yourself time to think through what you are going to say.
- If you struggle to stay still and just listen, try periodically asking questions about the topic the other person is talking about so you satisfy the urge to speak without drifting off from what the conversation was centered around.

SOCIAL SYNCHING IN YOUR ROMANTIC LIFE: WHY AWARENESS AND ACCEPTANCE OF YOUR ADHD IS CRUCIAL

It's highly unlikely for a romantic relationship to succeed or not feel toxic in the long term if your partner does not accept that you have ADHD.

It goes without saying that sharing that you have ADHD with your partner can be highly shameful and uncomfortable because it can feel like you are looking for excuses and admitting a fault in who you are. However, you can't deny that having ADHD is a significant part of who you are as a person. In much the same way that you wouldn't hide if you had a physical disability and needed a wheelchair, you can't hide or downplay the impact ADHD has on your life.

The first step toward a more ADHD-friendly and healthy relationship is educating yourself and your partner on how your brain is different and the way your ADHD symptoms affect your relationship. This condition can significantly affect your behavior, so it's crucial for your partner to realize that what you end up doing isn't always what you intended to do. Executive dysfunction, among other ADHD symptoms, creates a gap between what you want to do and what your brain allows you to do.

Understanding the context and underlying reason behind your actions is important so you treat each other with kindness, compassion, and non-judgmental curiosity. However, you still have the responsibility toward your partner and yourself to make an effort to better manage and accommodate your ADHD symptoms.

Your partner should offer you empathy and forgiveness when you struggle, but it's reasonable for them to gently nudge you to be better and try to find a better solution, strategy, and system to implement next time.

For example, forgetting one-third of the items you were supposed to buy from the grocery shop is understandable since forgetfulness is a huge part of the ADHD experience, but that doesn't mean you should just wave a white flag and admit defeat. Instead, next time, both of you can brainstorm solutions, like making a detailed list and updating it when you run out of specific items, so you know what you have to buy next time you go grocery shopping.

Second, you and your partner should distinguish between your symptoms and who you are as a person.

Failing to keep the home clean and forgetting important events doesn't make you "lazy" or "irresponsible." It's a result of your ADHD symptoms that you can both work toward improving. Using personality labels implies that your actions have done moral harm, where you intentionally decide to cause pain, stress, and discomfort to your partner, which couldn't be further from the truth.

Not only does it misinterpret the situation, but it's a counterproductive communication style. Using insults creates a feeling of isolation and alienation, where you defend yourself against someone else instead of working alongside them to find a suitable solution. The more alone and hurt you feel, the easier it becomes to keep pushing the other person away instead of reconciling, which can create a dangerous spiral. If you harbor pain and unprocessed emotions from previous conflicts, it's easier to get overly defensive, sensitive, and hurt over future disagreements or even neutral constructive conversations.

The only way to heal such wounds is to practice uninterrupted communication with one another. Both of you need to recognize your differences, especially if they don't have ADHD, and be fully willing to sit down, listen, and accept what the other is thinking and feeling without judgment, no matter how it makes you feel.

Listening involves a back-and-forth between you and your partner. First, one of you speaks and the other listens, and then the opposite, while in the meantime, you both make sure to paraphrase and express what you've understood to make sure you both are clear about the thoughts and feelings of the other person.

Finally, open and interrupted communication where you talk out anything should be your default way of conflict resolution, but it's okay for you to take time to cool off if intense and painful emotions are running high.

It's perfectly normal to say that you feel hurt and fear snapping at them unjustifiably, so you need to step out of the room for half an hour to calm yourself as long as you clearly communicate your needs instead of disappearing without an explanation. The difference between pausing an important conversation and chronically avoiding and running away from sensitive topics is that one is done strategically to calm your emotions and eventually talk it out, while the other is unhealthy avoidance that ends up creating more tension and anxiety instead of offering a resolution to what you both are concerned about.

CHAPTER 6
CRAFTING CALM FROM CHAOS ADHD-FRIENDLY ROUTINES FOR A STRESSFREE LIFE

Whether you realize it or not, almost all of your everyday decisions are automatic.

You don't put a lot of conscious effort in the morning when you go to the bathroom, make your coffee, prepare your clothes for the day, and quickly scramble to make breakfast out of the leftovers in the fridge.

This is completely natural and normal since your brain would quickly get overwhelmed and explode if you had to do a pros and cons analysis on the spot for every small step of the day. That would be impractical, inconvenient, and unsustainable.

You can't stop most of your decisions from being automatic throughout the day, but you have full control of what kinds of habits and routines eventually become your automatic actions.

This is why this chapter will do a deep dive into ADHD-friendly organizational solutions to help you create healthier, more meaningful, and sustainable routines.

HABIT STACKING: THE FOUNDATION OF DAILY TRIUMPHS

The science of habit-making is straightforward in theory. You want to pick a single activity, like guided meditation or gratitude journaling, and do it every single day. For a habit to stick, you want to do it at around the same time every day and need to find it relatively easy to do at your current level or to have easier versions for when you are not feeling motivated and productive.

When you pick habits, you want to do something that is certainly good for your well-being, mental health, and personal growth. The habits you do should also enhance your life by making symptoms of ADHD easier to manage. For example, meditation reduces stress but also trains your attention and impulse control.

Finally, you need to pick habits that you find personally meaningful. It's not enough to know that working out is "probably good for you" because everyone online says so. A personally meaningful habit is one for which you can easily give five reasons as to why you find it important to implement it in your life.

For instance, working out can:

- Get your mind off stressors and ongoing problems in your life
- Boost your mood and motivation for other activities
- Give your body strength and stamina that reduces aches and helps you heal from injuries
- Allows you a convenient way to meet up with friends who also want to pick up the habit
- Increases your confidence because you can see yourself progressing and getting better over time

Unfortunately, even if you try to follow all those steps, you are still likely to struggle when building a new habit or routine. It's common for people with ADHD to have an amazing week or two in the beginning, only to drop the habit entirely. Consistency is simply the hardest thing for an ADHD brain that craves variety, novelty, and excitement.

The unlikely solution we will offer in this section is habit stacking.

This is a type of habit-building where you combine a bunch of different activities and do them one after the other with short breaks in between.

Habit stacking sounds counterintuitive on the surface. Why would doing more help when you struggle to stick to the one habit you are trying to build? However, the technique has several unique advantages over regular habit building:

1. Instinctive Association: Doing habits one after the other creates a strong connection between them in your brain. This creates a strong craving to keep going and do the next action in line. For example, feeling the instinctive need to start running after you finish your dynamic stretches.
2. Building up Momentum: It's hard to get in the headspace for a 20-minute meditation session if you were just scrolling on your phone five minutes ago or just came back from work. However, washing your face with cold water, doing a short, slow breathing exercise, or listening to your affirmations all require significantly less effort, but it still primes you for the next action. By starting with easier habits, you warm yourself up and give yourself time to get in the headspace for the most intense habits.
3. Saves Time and Reduces Overwhelm: One huge problem with habit-building is that if you want to try creating more

than one habit at a time, you need to spend a lot of time warming up, getting yourself ready, and then making the habit. It's also overwhelming to look at in your schedule. Habit stacking simplifies the process because you only have one isolated chunk to go through in your schedule.
4. **The Ability to Hyper-Focus Reduces Action Paralysis:** Each time you do a different task, you have to switch contexts. The switch takes mental effort, which is why people with ADHD often experience action paralysis, struggling to start with the task even though they feel fully ready. Habit-stacking makes the process much easier because once you start, you keep doing the same thing instead of doing one habit in the morning, one in the afternoon, and one at dinner. You only need to struggle to start with a task once instead of multiple times.

Habit stacking is so intuitive that you may have been doing it without realizing it.

For example, when you wake up, drinking water, letting some sunlight into the room, making coffee, and going through your hygiene and skin routine is much easier than doing yoga, working out, meditating, or journaling since your mind and body are still lacking. Naturally, you start with what takes the least energy but still combine them all in a single time period.

There are also more minimalist versions of habit stacking that still take considerable time without switching between too many habits. For example, going for a walk after a meal to boost your metabolism and then doing guided meditation at the end while you are fed and energized from the light workout.

What you read are all suggestions of hypothetical routines, but what you end up trying is highly subjective.

Some people combine strength training with cardio in the end because it makes sense, while others are out of energy after an exhaustive dumbbell workout. Similarly, one group of people can seamlessly combine gratitude journaling with affirmations and meditation in the morning, while another can only meditate in the evening when they are winding down from the stressors of the day.

Creating your habit-stacking routine is a process of experimentation and trial and error. However, here are a few additional suggestions you may find helpful:

- Have an in-depth written version of your routine so you don't have to think about the next step.
- Forget about eating the frog and always start with the simplest and easiest-to-do habits to minimize procrastination.
- Try to always start your habits around the same time each day, or at least during the same part of the day (morning, noon, afternoon, evening).
- Make sure to schedule your day in a way that allows for sufficient time for your habit-stacking routine; otherwise, you can find excuses to skip it.
- Don't forget to celebrate and cherish your progress, even if it's small, because this gives you the motivation and momentum needed to keep going.

Finally, no matter what kind of habit-formation system you practice, reshaping your perception of consistency is important.

The neurotypical way of viewing consistency is showing up every day in some way, even if you are not doing as much. You already know that forcing your ADHD brain to switch context for a tiny bit can be unusually hard, even if you can technically do only a few minutes of a habit. Furthermore, some days, you will be terribly stressed and overwhelmed, making it impossible to even think about, let alone get yourself to make a specific habit.

So, consistency shouldn't be about showing up every single day but finding the strength to return after every single pause and break. Habit building is a life-long journey, and you will inevitably have days, weeks, and months where life gets in the way.

Following this approach allows you to reduce the shame of skipping days and avoid thinking that you might as well give up if you can't show up every single day.

TAILORING TASKS TO ENERGY LEVELS: WORK WITH YOUR ADHD, NOT AGAINST IT

Fluctuations in motivation and mental energy are common when you have ADHD. One day, you can crush your to-do list and even do a few extra chores, while tomorrow, you can struggle to climb out of bed, let alone worry about other tasks for the day.

This difference in concentration, alertness, and drive can also happen in different periods of the same day.

The official term for it is "chronotypes," which refers to the cycle of your body's biological clock (circadian rhythm). We call some people morning birds and other night owls due to the existence of chronotypes. Your chronotype will determine when you go to sleep and when you have the most energy during the day.

Here are a few strategies to optimize your work based on your energy level differences:

1. Create Different Routines Depending on Your Energy Levels: Meditating for 30 minutes a day would be ideal,

but most days, you may have the time and endurance for only 15 minutes or even five minutes. So, create three versions of each habit and routine you want to build. One for average days, which will be most of the time. One for exceptional days where you are full of motivation and energy, which will be the rarest. Finally, one for bad days, when you feel sick, highly exhausted, and on the verge of burnout, which would require you to do the bare minimum and go easy on yourself.
2. Learn about Your Chronotype: There are many free quizzes online, but you can also do a self-experiment by doing the same task across different times of the day. For example, try writing a blog post in the morning, noon, afternoon, early evening, and late at night, and you will see where you have the most energy based on the output you've produced. If you are working at times incompatible with your chronotype, you will feel exhausted, unmotivated, and resistant to working. Inversely, you will get in the flow more easily if you work within your chronotype's optimal periods. So, you can do highly mentally demanding and creative tasks at your peak and less exhausting tasks during your downtime.
3. Have Self-Compassion and Don't Be Afraid to Have Breaks: When you have an assignment or home chores to finish, it can be hard to convince yourself that you need to leave it for later. However, by beating yourself up and pushing despite struggling, the stress and overwhelm you create can actually sap the energy you'd have to try later. So, forgive yourself, and promise that the break is only temporary. Don't think of it as giving up but as a temporary pause needed to recharge and prepare yourself for later.

4. **Create Emergency Protocols When You Are Feeling Down:** Taking a break when you can't get any work done would be ideal, but that's not always an option when you have an urgent assignment. So, you can create short routines to get yourself back in the game. For example, wash your face with ice cold water, practice breath work for 20 repetitions with slow exhales, drink two cups of water, have a quick snack with carbs and protein, do some light exercises to get blood flowing, and turn on a set of favorite songs. As long as the short protocol helps to snap you out of your current headspace and rejuvenates your body and mind, it should be perfect.

In rare cases, your energy will not fluctuate in a clear pattern throughout the day, and you will feel exhausted and beaten down most days of the week. If you feel like average energy and motivation levels are the most you get all day and dread doing many of the tasks you have to do, you may be on the verge or in the middle of a burnout episode.

If you have a hunch about burnout, you will need to reflect and see whether you are more irritable and cynical than usual and if you have physical symptoms, like a loss of appetite, brain fog, or regular headaches. Also, reflect if you more frequently turn toward coping mechanisms, like alcohol, video games, social media, TV entertainment, and other quick sources of pleasure and escapism.

Knowing whether you are in a slump because it's just not a productive day or you are in the middle of a burnout episode is crucial because it will completely change how you respond.

First, a burnout episode means you should do only the bare minimum required and avoid tasks that are not highly urgent. I know that only some are privileged to clock out and mind their business after their nine-to-five or have enough free time during the weekend, but take every opportunity you have to rest by going for walks in nature, avoiding social media, turning off work notifications, and spending time with your current hobbies and passions. This emphasis on rest should be your priority for the upcoming weeks.

Second, healing burnout will require you to do some digging to discover the underlying cause (toxic friendships or work environment, an overwhelming amount of workload, doing work not aligned with your values, etc.) so you can work on removing it from your life long-term. It goes without saying that you can't change a huge aspect of your life overnight, like your social circle or employment status, but you can take a lot of small steps on the side to slowly transition toward a less stressful and mentally damaging environment.

THE ROLE OF MORNING ROUTINES IN GETTING YOU STARTED FOR THE DAY

Morning routines are the most commercialized and mainstream popular forms of habit-building. Influencers often describe how they wake up at 5 am and go through an exhaustive list of activities from sauna and cold showers to HIIT workouts and running.

This is not realistic or sustainable for the average person. After all, waking up extra early to "prepare for the day" isn't worth it if the lack of adequate sleep tanks your performance. Furthermore, the average person who works a typical nine-to-five does not have the luxury of an extensive routine in the morning.

Let's bring back the theme of minimalism and functionality.

You shouldn't include anything in your morning routine if it isn't essential to your daily functioning. For instance, stretching, gratitude journaling, and practicing breathwork techniques would be nice, but they won't significantly impact your performance, especially if you have done all those habits in a rush due to the lack of time.

So, don't feel pressured to have a morning routine just for the sake of having a morning routine. It's perfectly normal to do the bare minimum, like washing yourself, hydrating, making yourself coffee, and then getting to work. It would be even better if you skipped some of the steps by preparing them the night before, like getting your clothes, backpack, and breakfast cooked or ready to be cooked the night before.

Excessively long morning routines could actually be hurting your productivity, especially if you are working from home. It's one thing to have a routine to wake yourself up better and get ready for work. However, having an excessively long morning routine can actually be used as a form of procrastination to delay getting started with the most important work of the day.

EVENING WIND DOWN: PREPARING FOR TOMORROW

Your sleeping routine is important because it determines your performance for the following day. Sleep deprivation, or a lack of sufficient high-quality sleep, leads to worse impulse control, reduced concentration, increased mood swings, and lowered motivation.

It's easy to neglect creating a night routine because you are tired, and brainlessly browsing social media, binge-watching TV shows, or playing video games is much more tempting.

The total opposite could also be true. Many ADHD-ers get a sudden burst of energy as the sun goes down because they are natural night owls. They could prefer the nighttime due to the reduced noise and distractions, or just the reduced time before bed creates an intense urgency to over-compensate for falling behind earlier.

Here are a few strategies you can implement for a robust night routine:

1. Draw the Line between Working and Non-Working Parts of the Day: If you are serious about a winding off routine, pick a time when you want your working day to end, like 6 or 7 pm. This will suck in the beginning. You will have days when your energy comes right up when you have to stop working, but you should stick with it unless your work is urgent. By making it impossible to work after a certain hour, you create urgency in the earlier parts of the day and reduce the excuses you can make for skipping the night routine.
2. Cut off Social Media during the Night: Social media and internet surfing are the opposite of what your brain needs at night. The highly intense stimulation, blue light from the screen, and the endless ability to get you down rabbit holes and satisfy random questions you have are all a trap that's hard to escape. There's nothing wrong with browsing while eating or during breaks at work, but try to allocate your time in the earlier parts of the day.
3. Balance between Boredom and Excessive Stimulation: If you are dying from boredom, you will return to habits you shouldn't be doing at night. However, if you are highly stimulated, like when working out, playing video games, or watching scary movies, then your cortisol levels spike, and it's hard to relax. Instead, you can try guided meditation, yoga, book reading, or anything else that's fun but not enough to hyper-focus to the point it breaks your structure. Finally, make sure to have variety in your

activities because repetition is much more likely to get boring.

4. **Prepare For the Next Day:** You can prepare meals and ingredients for tomorrow, plan out the day, prepare a to-do list, and get your clothes, backpack, purse, and anything else you need for tomorrow. This can help you burn off any remaining energy you have at the end of the day and give you more confidence that you are prepared for tomorrow, which is especially reassuring if you feel as though you haven't done enough today.

Winding down is only one part of a proper night routine. It's equally important to learn how to fall asleep. After all, you could have had the most optimal and perfect sequence of relaxing activities before going to bed and still struggle to fall asleep.

People with ADHD tend to struggle to fall asleep at night, struggle with restless sleep in which they often wake up, and have difficulty waking up in the morning. Alongside sleep disruptions, cases of insomnia are also highly common when you have ADHD.[1]

There is no conclusion on the exact underlying cause, but there are a couple of theories. First, having ADHD can lead to disruptions in your circadian rhythm, so you are more likely to be a night owl and struggle to fall asleep before 2 am. Second, internal hyperactivity, the endless thoughts violently spinning in your brain, and emotional dysregulation make it harder to keep your brain calm and relaxed. Finally, perfectionism and feelings of inadequacy can increase rumination during the night or attempts to compensate by working late.

No matter the cause, sleep disruptions create a vicious cycle. Once you stop sleeping enough, your ADHD symptoms grow worse, so it becomes harder to stay productive, do your night routine, and keep yourself calm.

No matter the underlying cause, here are a few strategies that can help combat this sleep disruption:

1. Keep Your Sleeping Hours Consistent: Your circadian rhythm gives a significant but often neglected hint about what your body wants: routine and consistency. Trying to go to sleep and wake up at approximately the same time every day gives your body a cue to prepare you for sleep and wakefulness during a specific hour. It can be challenging in the beginning, but before long, falling asleep will become automatic.
2. Exercise throughout the Day: The more physically beaten down you are, the more your body craves sleep for recovery and the less energy you have to spare on overthinking and rumination during the night. Working out prior to bed can have the opposite effect, so it's an excellent idea to get as much movement as possible throughout the day. Not everyone has the opportunity or energy for a two-hour strength session and 30-minute cardio, but going for a short walk at lunch, pacing around during the day, and scheduling sport-based activities throughout the week with friends are all accessible options.
3. Be Mindful of What You Are Putting in Your Body: First, alcohol consumption will disrupt your sleep because it's dehydrating and interrupts your ability for deep sleep (the most restorative part of the sleep cycle). Second, not drinking water for two hours will make it easier to avoid waking up during the night. Third, you may want to adjust your dietary patterns in the hours before sleep. If you wake

up at 3 to 4 am and feel hungry, you may need to snack a bit before a meal or have more nutrient-dense meals rich in protein throughout the day. However, if your meals are highly caloric, you may want to avoid eating three to four hours before bed to let your metabolism rest. Finally, this will hurt, but you need to reduce coffee since caffeine can remain in your system for up to 12 to 14 hours, depending on your metabolic rate. So, keep it to two cups maximum, and don't drink in the afternoon at the latest.

4. **Reduce Your Exposure to Blue Light in the Evening:** Your body can't distinguish between light coming from your TV, phone, or laptop and the light from the sun. Your circadian rhythm signals your body to fall asleep when blue light exposure is significantly reduced because it assumes the sun has gone down. So, by taking a break from sources of such light one to two hours before bed, you can fall asleep faster. You can go cold turkey and avoid electronic devices altogether, or reduce the brightness and install blue light filter apps on your phone, laptop, and computer.

5. **Lower Your Body Temperature:** Your circadian rhythm is influenced by daylight and the temperature around you. The colder it is, preferably enough to reduce your core temperature by 2 to 3 degrees Fahrenheit or 1 degree Celsius, the easier it is to fall asleep. After all, nobody can deny that snuggling in a warm blanket during the winter is much more comfortable than sleeping almost naked during the summer. Opening the window, turning down the AC, and avoiding taking hot showers or moving a lot before bed are all great ways to keep your body temperature low and prepare for better sleep.

6. **Consider Meditation:** Guided meditation using a YouTube video or an app or just silent meditation by yourself is one

of the best ways to fall asleep. In a meditative state, you focus on an anchor point, like your breathing, which naturally teaches you to resist impulses, like checking your phone or getting back to work. You also ground yourself, becoming more aware of your physical exhaustion and reducing rumination and over-thinking. Meditating calms your nervous system by reducing anxiety and stress levels, which signals to your body that it cannot only relax but also rest and sleep.

Thinking you need to do everything we described above can be overwhelming. This can create anxiety and, eventually, avoidance because you dread putting yourself through so much. So, instead of trying to implement it all at once, take baby steps by experimenting with only one suggestion, like cutting screen time before sleep and incorporating movement throughout the day. Before long, you will pick up momentum and find more motivation to expand on the progress you are already making.

GIVE OTHERS THE START THEY ARE SEEKING

I hope this book continues to be a companion throughout your lifetime and that once in a while, you pick it up to receive useful reminders of how to keep your home, desk, and shared spaces clutter-free. I can envision you creating your very own habit-stacking routine and cherishing every step taken in the right direction, no matter how small it may be. Remember that the aim is never perfection, but rather, proactivity. By spending just a little time every day on your routine, you can ensure that clutter never piles up to such an extent that it becomes overwhelming.

If you feel that you can now transform tidiness into a habit, kindly leave a sentence or two, so other people with ADHD know where to find a book on decluttering that is catered to them. That's the great thing about having a tidy home… it puts you in a focused frame of mind and enables you to think of important things like how you can pay it forward and help others in need.

Thanks for your support. May the information you found in this book continue to help you throughout your lifetime, so that your home becomes an oasis of peace and comfort.

Scan the QR code below:

CONCLUSION

The typical ADHD diagnosis story goes something like this: Your life is in total chaos, you learn about ADHD and decide to get diagnosed, everything turns around, and suddenly, you get your life together and begin to thrive.

Unfortunately, my brain must have missed the memo of what it was supposed to do after my official diagnosis. One week after that day, I was bawling my eyes out on the kitchen floor after my grocery shopping trip.

Half an hour before my meltdown, I realized I had forgotten to close the car door again. I also bought too much unnecessary junk food, didn't get everything from my shopping list, and forgot to clean the fridge of the rotting fruits and veggies before shopping. The horror got only worse when I tried to cook, only to end up overwhelmed.

Before I knew it, my body had sunk to the ground, and I was aggressively trembling while crying my eyes out. I felt sad and hopeless, but there was also immense anger and frustration with myself. If I wasn't whispering it out loud, you bet I was internally thinking how lazy, careless, and irresponsible I was being once again.

Once the negative-thought train picked up pace, it didn't stop for hours. I was angry at myself. Then, I became furious at my ADHD diagnosis for not magically fixing me and giving me false hopes of getting better. Before long, I was cursing my ADHD and promising myself that I would work harder next time and stop using it as an excuse.

I calmed down by the next day, but this wasn't the first or last of my fiery tantrums and intense episodes. It turned out that accepting my ADHD and learning to live with it was much more than the brief catharsis you feel once you finally get diagnosed.

For much longer after my diagnosis, I kept blaming my personality instead of acknowledging my ADHD as a significant factor. From a young age, I was taught to take absolute and full responsibility for all my actions. So, how could a grown woman blame the chaos in her home on the wrong brain chemical cocktail in her head?

I was afraid of turning my ADHD from an explanation to an excuse, and this fear wouldn't leave me for many years. So, I had all I needed to get better, but I had to fight my conflicting beliefs and resolve the cognitive dissonance I was going through.

So, I want you to know that it's okay to know what you should be doing, but you are still struggling. I don't expect you to go through my whole book and suddenly turn your life around at once. Unfortunately, life is too complicated for that to happen.

The demon I fought was my persistent denial and reluctance to accept my ADHD, but your battle will likely be different. I know people who:

- Struggle with intense sensory overload and a packed schedule that leaves little time and energy for cleaning and de-cluttering
- Struggle with childhood trauma associated with organization and cleaning, making it hard for them to enjoy the process
- Struggle with terrible perfectionism and always strive to do as much as possible, even if they need to do much less to be functional

So, adjust your expectations, and always remember you are not alone. Even if everyone's problems are not exactly the same, you should know that we all have lives so complex that simply knowing what to do isn't enough to actually do it.

You will likely read this book, try to implement a few strategies, get some moderate success, and then forget about it for two months as life gets in the way. Then, you will likely re-read it a few more times, implementing a few strategies each time, before using it as a reference when facing an organizational dilemma. That's how I imagine most people will realistically interact with this book.

It's not perfect, but it's good enough. We are humans, not robots designed to maximize productivity. So, have some self-compassion and patience, and be kinder to yourself.

No matter your organizational challenge, real progress is not how quickly you try to make the problem go away but how much you keep trying, no matter the setbacks and struggles you experience.

ENDNOTES

INTRODUCTION

1. Spaulding, S. L., K. Fruitman, E. Rapoport, D. Soled, and A. Adesman. "Impact of ADHD on Household Chores." *Journal of Attention Disorders* 25, no. 10 (2021): 1374-1383.
2. Niermann, Hannah C. M., and Anouk Scheres. "The Relation between Procrastination and Symptoms of Attention-Deficit Hyperactivity Disorder (ADHD) in Undergraduate Students." *International Journal of Methods in Psychiatric Research* (December 2014). https://www.ncbi.nlm.nih.gov/pmc/articles/PMC6878228/.

1. DECODING ADHD-THE SCIENCE AND THE STORIES

1. Stolte, Marije, et al. "Characterizing Creative Thinking and Creative Achievements in Relation to Symptoms of Attention-Deficit/Hyperactivity Disorder and Autism Spectrum Disorder." *Frontiers in Psychiatry* (July 1, 2022). https://www.ncbi.nlm.nih.gov/pmc/articles/PMC9283685/.
2. Katusic, Maja Z., et al. "Attention-Deficit Hyperactivity Disorder in Children with High Intelligence Quotient: Results from a Population-Based Study." *Journal of Developmental and Behavioral Pediatrics* (2011). https://www.ncbi.nlm.nih.gov/pmc/articles/PMC3095845/.
3. "ADHD, IQ, and Giftedness." YouTube video, 23 June 2023. https://www.youtube.com/watch?v=4_BIaLhdkrw.
4. Barrett, K. K. "ADHD and the Case for Support through Collegiate Age: Understanding the Lifecycle of Developmental Delays in Executive Function for ADHD and its Impact on Goal Setting." *Journal of Child Development Disorders* 4, 11 (2018). DOI: 10.4172/2472-1786.100074.
5. Arnsten, Amy F. T. "The Emerging Neurobiology of Attention Deficit Hyperactivity Disorder: The Key Role of the Prefrontal Association Cortex." *The Journal of Pediatrics* (May 1, 2009). https://www.ncbi.nlm.nih.gov/pmc/articles/PMC2894421/.
6. Grimm, Oliver, et al. "Genetics of ADHD: What Should the Clinician Know?" *Current Psychiatry Reports* (February 27, 2020). https://www.ncbi.nlm.nih.gov/pmc/articles/PMC7046577/.
7. Ibid.
8. Pinto, Sofia, et al. "Eating Patterns and Dietary Interventions in ADHD: A Narrative Review." *Nutrients* (October 16, 2022). https://www.ncbi.nlm.nih.gov/pmc/articles/PMC9608000/.

9. Dinu, Larisa M., et al. "The Effects of Different Exercise Approaches on Attention Deficit Hyperactivity Disorder in Adults: A Randomised Controlled Trial." *Behavioral Sciences* (February 2, 2023). https://www.ncbi.nlm.nih.gov/pmc/articles/PMC9952527/.
10. Community Health Centers of Southern Iowa. (n.d.). *ADHD DSM-5 checklist*. Retrieved from https://chsciowa.org/sites/chsciowa.org/files/resource/files/1_-_adhd_dsm-5_checklist.pdf
11. Advokat, Claire, and Mindy Scheithauer. "Attention-Deficit Hyperactivity Disorder (ADHD) Stimulant Medications as Cognitive Enhancers." *Frontiers in Neuroscience* (May 29, 2013). https://www.ncbi.nlm.nih.gov/pmc/articles/PMC3666055/.
12. Budur, Kumar, et al. "Non-Stimulant Treatment for Attention Deficit Hyperactivity Disorder." *Psychiatry* (July 2005). https://www.ncbi.nlm.nih.gov/pmc/articles/PMC3000197/.
13. Knouse, Laura E., and Steven A Safren. "Current Status of Cognitive Behavioral Therapy for Adult Attention-Deficit Hyperactivity Disorder." *The Psychiatric Clinics of North America* (September 2010). https://www.ncbi.nlm.nih.gov/pmc/articles/PMC2909688/.
14. Niermann, Hannah C. M., and Anouk Scheres. "The Relation between Procrastination and Symptoms of Attention-Deficit Hyperactivity Disorder (ADHD) in Undergraduate Students." *International Journal of Methods in Psychiatric Research* (December 2014). https://www.ncbi.nlm.nih.gov/pmc/articles/PMC6878228/.
15. Munawar, K., et al. "Acceptance and Commitment Therapy for Individuals Having Attention Deficit Hyperactivity Disorder (ADHD): A Scoping Review." *Heliyon*. https://pubmed.ncbi.nlm.nih.gov/34466706/.
16. Mehren, Aylin, et al. "Physical Exercise in Attention Deficit Hyperactivity Disorder - Evidence and Implications for the Treatment of Borderline Personality Disorder." *Borderline Personality Disorder and Emotion Dysregulation* (January 6, 2020). https://www.ncbi.nlm.nih.gov/pmc/articles/PMC6945516/.
17. Villagomez, Amelia, and Ujjwal Ramtekkar. "Iron, Magnesium, Vitamin D, and Zinc Deficiencies in Children Presenting with Symptoms of Attention-Deficit/Hyperactivity Disorder." *Children* (September 29, 2014). https://www.ncbi.nlm.nih.gov/pmc/articles/PMC4928738/.
18. Colten, Harvey R. "Extent and Health Consequences of Chronic Sleep Loss and Sleep Disorders." In *Sleep Disorders and Sleep Deprivation: An Unmet Public Health Problem* (January 1, 1970). https://www.ncbi.nlm.nih.gov/books/NBK19961/.
19. Ghanizadeh, Ahmad. "Sensory Processing Problems in Children with ADHD, a Systematic Review." *Psychiatry Investigation* (June 2011). https://www.ncbi.nlm.nih.gov/pmc/articles/PMC3149116/.
20. Ptacek, Radek, et al. "Clinical Implications of the Perception of Time in Attention Deficit Hyperactivity Disorder (ADHD): A Review." *Medical Science Monitor* (May 26, 2019). https://www.ncbi.nlm.nih.gov/pmc/articles/PMC6556068/.
21. Philipsen, Alexandra, et al. "Attention Deficit Hyperactivity Disorder in Adult-

hood: Diagnosis, Etiology and Therapy." *Deutsches Arzteblatt International* (April 2008). https://www.ncbi.nlm.nih.gov/pmc/articles/PMC2696867/.
22. Dodson, William, M.D. "New Insights into Rejection Sensitive Dysphoria." *ADDitude* (December 20, 2023). https://www.additudemag.com/rejection-sensitive-dysphoria-adhd-emotional-dysregulation/.
23. "The Important Role of Executive Functioning and Self-Regulation in ADHD." Russell A. Barkley. https://www.russellbarkley.org/factsheets/ADHD_EF_and_SR.pdf.
24. "Apa PsycNet." American Psychological Association, 2024. https://psycnet.apa.org/record/2014-57877-003.
25. Ashinoff, Brandon K., and Ahmad Abu-Akel. "Hyperfocus: The Forgotten Frontier of Attention." *Psychological Research* (February 2021). https://www.ncbi.nlm.nih.gov/pmc/articles/PMC7851038/.
26. Stolte, Marije, et al. "Characterizing Creative Thinking and Creative Achievements in Relation to Symptoms of Attention-Deficit/Hyperactivity Disorder and Autism Spectrum Disorder." *Frontiers in Psychiatry* (July 1, 2022). https://www.ncbi.nlm.nih.gov/pmc/articles/PMC9283685/.
27. Lerner, Daniel A., et al. "Entrepreneurship and Attention Deficit/Hyperactivity Disorder: A Large-Scale Study Involving the Clinical Condition of ADHD." *Small Business Economics* (May 15, 2018). https://link.springer.com/article/10.1007/s11187-018-0061-1.

2. THE CHAOS OF CLUTTER NAVIGATING ADHD'S ORGANIZATIONAL MINEFIELD

1. "Childhood ADHD Symptoms in Relation to Trauma." https://journals.sagepub.com/doi/abs/10.1177/1063426620982624.

3. ROOM BY ROOM REBOOT CUSTOM ORGANIZING FOR EVERY SPACE

1. Akin, Sumeyye, et al. "Processed Meat Products and Snacks Consumption in ADHD: A Case-Control Study." *Northern Clinics of Istanbul* (July 8, 2022). https://www.ncbi.nlm.nih.gov/pmc/articles/PMC9464840/.
2. Contreras, Raian E., et al. "Physiological and Epigenetic Features of Yoyo Dieting and Weight Control." *Frontiers in Genetics* (December 11, 2019). https://www.ncbi.nlm.nih.gov/pmc/articles/PMC6917653/.

4. DECLUTTER YOUR DESK, OPTIMIZE YOUR WORKING STATION TO REDUCE STRESS AND ENHANCE PRODUCTIVITY WITH ADHD-FRIENDLY PLANNING

1. Zhang, Na, et al. "Effects of Dehydration and Rehydration on Cognitive Performance and Mood among Male College Students in Cangzhou, China: A

Self-Controlled Trial." *International Journal of Environmental Research and Public Health* (May 29, 2019). https://www.ncbi.nlm.nih.gov/pmc/articles/PMC6603652/.
2. Wheeler, Michael J., et al. "Sedentary Behavior as a Risk Factor for Cognitive Decline? A Focus on the Influence of Glycemic Control in Brain Health." *Alzheimer's & Dementia* (New York, N.Y.) (May 2, 2017). https://www.ncbi.nlm.nih.gov/pmc/articles/PMC5651418/.

6. CRAFTING CALM FROM CHAOS ADHD-FRIENDLY ROUTINES FOR A STRESSFREE LIFE

1. Surman, Craig B. H., and Daniel M. Walsh. "Managing Sleep in Adults with ADHD: From Science to Pragmatic Approaches." *Brain Sciences* (October 16, 2021). https://www.ncbi.nlm.nih.gov/pmc/articles/PMC8534229/.

Made in the USA
Monee, IL
13 January 2025